lonely planet

VENICE
ENCOUNTER

ALISON BING

Venice Encounter
1st edition · January 2009

Published by Lonely Planet Publications Pty Ltd
ABN 36 005 607 983

Australia	Head Office, Locked Bag 1
	Footscray, Vic 3011
	☎ 03 8379 8000 fax 03 8379 8111
	talk2us@lonelyplanet.com.au
USA	150 Linden St, Oakland, CA 94607
	☎ 510 250 6400
	toll free 800 275 8555
	fax 510 893 8572
	info@lonelyplanet.com
UK	2nd fl, 186 City Rd
	London EC1V 2NT
	☎ 020 7106 2100 fax 020 7106 2101
	go@lonelyplanet.co.uk

This title was commissioned in Lonely Planet's London office and produced by: **Commissioning Editor** Paula Hardy **Coordinating Editor** Laura Stansfeld **Coordinating Cartographer** Amanda Sierp **Layout Designer** David Kemp **Assisting Editor** Janet Austin **Assisting Cartographer** Joanne Luke **Managing Editor** Imogen Bannister **Managing Cartographer** Mark Griffiths **Cover Designer** Vicki Beale **Project Manager** Ruth Cosgrove **Managing Layout Designers** Laura Jane, Celia Wood **Thanks to** Shahara Ahmed, Jennifer Garrett, Lisa Knights, Trent Paton, Lyahna Spencer

ISBN 978 1 74104 997 8

Printed by Hang Tai Printing Company.
Printed in China.

Acknowledgement Venice Vaporetto map © Actv SpA 2008

HOW TO USE THIS BOOK
Colour-Coding & Maps

Colour-coding is used for symbols on maps and in the text that they relate to (eg all eating venues on the maps and in the text are given a green knife and fork symbol). Each *sestiere* (neighbourhood) also gets its own colour, and this is used down the edge of the page and throughout that neighbourhood section.

Prices

Multiple prices listed with reviews (eg €10/5 or €10/5/20) indicate adult/child, adult/concession or adult/child/family.

Send us your feedback We love to hear from readers — your comments help make our books better. We read every word you send us, and we always guarantee that your feedback goes straight to the appropriate authors. The most useful submissions are rewarded with a free book. To send us your updates and find out about Lonely Planet events, newsletters and travel news visit our award-winning website: *lonelyplanet.com/contact*.

Note: We may edit, reproduce and incorporate your comments in Lonely Planet products such as guidebooks, websites and digital products, so let us know if you don't want your comments reproduced or your name acknowledged. For a copy of our privacy policy visit *lonelyplanet.com/privacy*.

ALISON BING

When not scribbling notes in church pews and
methodically eating her way across Venice, Alison
contributes to Lonely Planet's *Italy, Milan* and
Tuscany & Umbria guides, as well as architecture,
food and art glossies such as *Architectural Record,
Cooking Light* and Italy's *Flash Art*. Currently she
divides her time between San Francisco and a
hilltop town on the border of Lazio and Tuscany
with partner (and fellow Slow Food member)
Marco Flavio Marinucci. Alison holds a bachelor's
degree in art history and a masters degree from
the Fletcher School of Law and Diplomacy, a
joint program between Tufts and Harvard Universities, but she regularly
undermines these perfectly respectable diplomatic credentials with opin-
ionated culture commentary for newspapers, magazines and radio.

ALISON'S THANKS

Complimenti e grazie tanto a Susanna Sent, Davide Amadio, Francesco e
Matteo Pinto, Rosanna Corró, Cristina della Toffola, Giovanni d'Este and
Cristina Bottero of the Venice Tourism Office. *Mille grazie e baccione alla
mia famiglia a Roma e Stateside*, the Bings, Ferrys and Marinuccis;
como sempre to fearless leader and fellow traveller Paula Hardy, and to
dauntless cartographers Mark Griffiths and Amanda Sierp; a thunderous
brava! for editor Laura Stansfeld; *ma sopra tutto* to Marco Flavio Marinucci, who makes it all worthwhile.

This book is dedicated to *voáltri venexiani,* who keep the city and its
spirits afloat.

Our readers Many thanks to the travellers who wrote to us with helpful hints, useful advice and interesting anecdotes.
Christian Aagaard, Catherine Linton, Lorna Smith, Jessica Sturman

Photographs p52, p76, p93, p116, p129, p143 by Alison Bing; p12, p16 The Bridgeman Art Library; p17 Elisabetta
Villa/Getty Images; p18 Alberto Pizzoli/AFP/Getty Images; p20 Patrick Hertzog/AFP/Getty Images; p29 Christophe Simon/
AFP/Getty Images. All other photographs by Lonely Planet Images, and by Krzysztof Dydynski except p68 Diana Mayfield; p30-
Roberto Soncin Gerometta; p102 John Hay; p156 Karl Blackwell; p126 Richard Cummins; p144 Greg Elms; p138 Jon Davison;
p31 Holger Leue; p21, p32 (top left), p34, p118, p160, p163 Brent Winebrenner; p8, p14, p19, p27, p57, p99, p130 Juliet
Coombe. **Cover photograph** Gondolier paddling along a canal, Gary Yeowell/Getty Images.

All images are copyright of the photographers unless otherwise indicated. Many of the images in this guide are available for
licensing from **Lonely Planet Images:** www.lonelyplanetimages.com.

Bow to the inevitable and take a gorgeous gondola ride (p175)

CONTENTS

THIS IS VENICE

As you approach the portals of the Basilica di San Marco, you feel a buzz surge through the crowd. A moment ago, you were a motley group of tourists, art students and the occasional nun – now you're ensemble players in the epic drama that is Venice.

Yet Venice isn't a one-stage venue. The dazzling pageantry continues at I Frari, Gallerie dell'Accademia, Scuola Grande di San Rocco and, of course, Teatro La Fenice. And if you think your walk-on part at these attractions is exhilarating, wait until you step backstage – which is never more than a *sotoportego* (passageway) away. In narrow *calli* (streets) off the thoroughfares to San Marco, you'll glimpse the behind-the-scenes creativity that keeps the whole production afloat: artisans at work in their studios, cooks whipping up four-star *cicheti* (Venetian tapas) on single-burner hotplates, musicians lugging 18th-century cellos to chamber-music practice. Here the volume is turned down, and you can hear the muffled sounds of intermission – neighbours kissing hello and Veronese spaniels trotting over footbridges.

But haven't Venetians heard their city is sinking? Absolutely – and true to form, they're staging a creative comeback. Venice has already survived plague, invasion and floods; under threat of imminent destruction, Venetians painted masterpieces, invented new architecture styles and created new musical genres. But rising tides are one thing, cruise ships are another. Millions of visitors annually disembark with just three hours to tour Venice, and if each day tripper asked one local for directions to San Marco, every Venetian would hear the question repeated 333 times a year.

This is where you come in. With your excellent map and insider info, ask questions Venetians actually enjoy answering. What's the best Venetian dish? How about those Venice Film Festival winners? And the most revealing question of all: what's new? Already there are new twists on baroque music, new galleries in ancient warehouses and new hotels in Palladian cloisters. Your timing is perfect – Venice's next act is just beginning.

Top left Gain a new perspective on the Campanile di San Marco (p44) **Top right** Wooden, me? Try to outstare the mannequins at Fiorella Gallery (p48) **Bottom** Gondolas? Check. Stripy shirt? Check. It must be Venice.

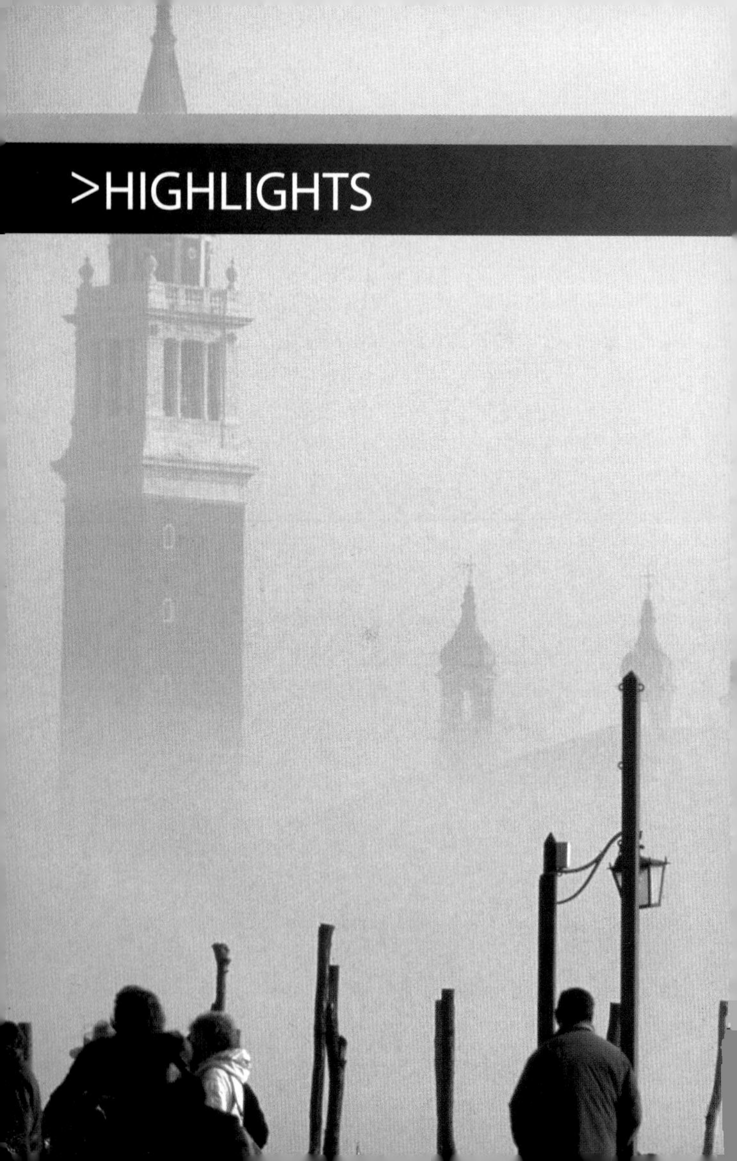

Morning mists shroud Piazza San Marco (p40)

>1 BASILICA DI SAN MARCO

PREPARE TO BE WOWED BY THE BASILICA DI SAN MARCO

The burning question isn't *if* you should see Venice's jewel of a cathedral, but when. Morning mystics insist you must arrive when millions of sunlit tesserae emit an otherworldly glow, causing jaws to drop to the semiprecious-stone floors. Sunset romantics lobby you to linger in the Piazza San Marco, waiting for the fading sun to shatter portal mosaics into golden shards as the Caffè Florian house band strikes up the tango. Our advice? Go now, and go often. With millennium-old special-effects wizardry that puts modern Hollywood to shame, the basilica is set to dazzle morning to night, inside and out.

This landmark was inspired by religious larceny in 828, when Venetian merchants smuggled the corpse of St Matthew out of Egypt. Venice already had all the makings of a global trading centre – plenty of ports, a defendable position against Charlemagne and the Huns, a patron saint to oversee transactions – but there was no glorious landmark to fix Venice's place on the world map. And so the city summoned the best artisans from Byzantium and beyond to enshrine both the relic and Venice's trading prowess in one unmistakable monument.

But there remained the small matter of construction. The usual medieval setbacks of riots and fires thrice destroyed exterior mosaics and weakened the underlying structure. As ceilings drooped and tastes changed, Jacopo Sansovino and other church architects grafted on

TOP FIVE SAN MARCO MUST SEES

> Cupola of the Ascension — the golden central dome is truly uplifting, with angels swirling overhead and a dreamy-eyed St Mark on the pendentive (dome support).
> Pala d'Oro — minutely worked enamel portraits of apostles in superhero capes outshine the 2000 gemstones on this priceless altarpiece.
> Dome of Genesis — created 650 years before abstract art and hip hop, these medieval mosaics show the separation of sky and water, and angels busting dance moves.
> Pavimenti — prepare to be floored by the dizzying optical effects of polychrome stone mosaics.
> Loggia dei Cavalli — bronze horses leap off the balcony over Piazza San Marco.

supports, Gothic arches and every type of polychrome marble avail-able for purchase or pillage. Occasionally higher purpose got clouded over by construction dust: St Mark's bones were misplaced twice.

Give or take a holy tibia, Venice's transition from backwater upstart to sophisticated cosmopolitan capital was successfully completed by the 18th century. Today, even during the high tides that wash over the sinking piazza, San Marco still sets the high-water mark for architectural amazement.

See p41 for more information.

>2 GALLERIE DELL'ACCADEMIA

HEAD TO THE ACCADEMIA FOR ART THAT'S CAUSED CENTURIES OF SCANDAL AND SENSATION

Somewhere in the queue to enter the Accademia, you may grumpily wonder if the wait is worthwhile. But when the masses of students part to reveal Andrea Mantegna's 1466 haughtily handsome *St George* or Rosalba Carriera's brutally honest self-portrait from 1730, you'll get the thrill of locking eyes with a major celebrity across a crowded room.

The Accademia is hardly strictly academic – it also holds all the un-forgettable characters, tall tales, murderous intrigue and juicy scandals that could be expected from the most extreme Venetian dinner parties. Giovanni Bellini's gorgeous Madonna is haloed by red cher-

---

TOP FIVE PORTRAITS THAT LOOK ALIVE
> Giorgione's *Old Woman*
> Hans Memling's *Portrait of a Young Man*
> Gentile Bellini's *Blessed Lorenzo Giustinian*
> Giambattista Piazzetta's *Fortune-Teller*
> Lorenzo Lotto's *Portrait of a Young Scholar*

ubs glowing like XXX neon signs, while a bejewelled beauty in the corner steals the Madonna's thunder in Titian's *Mary's Presentation in the Temple*. Tintoretto's Old Testament account of God's creation of the animals is suspiciously Venetian, with its spotlighted lions (the symbol of St Mark) and mutant lagoon fish that would definitely be sold at a discount at the Pescheria. Giambattista Tiepolo's *Miracle of the Bronze Serpent* is cracked from when it was hastily rolled up by creeped-out viewers, but for sheer, shimmering gore, there's no topping Vittore Carpaccio's *Crucifixion and Glorification of the Ten Thousand Martyrs of Mount Ararat*. Suffice to say, Harry's Bar was quite correct in naming a dish of bloody raw beef after this painter.

But the most controversial scene stealer is Paolo Veronese's *Feast in the House of Levi* (pictured above), which was called *The Last Supper* until Inquisition leaders condemned Veronese for showing drunkards, dwarves, dogs and even Reformation-minded Germans cavorting amid the apostles. Veronese refused to change a thing besides the title, and Venice stood by this act of artistic defiance. Follow the exchanges, gestures and eye contact among the characters here, and you'll notice that not one Moorish trader, stumbling servant, gambler or bright-eyed lapdog could have been painted over without losing an essential piece of the puzzle – and not coincidentally, the same can be said of Venice.

See p113 for more information.

HIGHLIGHTS

>3 OPEN-AIR MARKETS

FIND ALL THE FIXINGS FOR VENICE'S SIGNATURE DISHES AT THE CITY'S MARKETS

Cutting-edge restaurants worldwide are catching on to something Venetians have known for 600 years: food tastes better when it's fresh, seasonal and local. The Pescheria (Fish Market; p94) is any foodie's first stop in Venice – especially for *moscardino* (baby octopus), crabs ranging from tiny *moeche* (soft-shell crabs) to *granseole* (spider crabs), and *seppie* (squid) of all sizes.

Compared to the tame specimens you'd find at your average supermarket, the indigenous Veneto fare at the Rialto produce markets (p94) and on canalside stalls (p95) looks like it just landed from another planet. Tiny purplish *castraure* (baby artichokes) could be shrunken alien heads, white Bassano asparagus is eerily spectral and red radicchio di Treviso looks like a mutant flower from Mars. Even familiar food goes wild here: suggestively shaped tomatoes and red capsicum seem very fresh indeed, and those saucy little strawberries could make grown men cry.

>4 TINTORETTO

CHASE LIGHTNING FLASHES OF INSIGHT THROUGH TINTORETTO'S STORMY SCENES

Lightning bolts can scarcely keep up with Tintoretto's loaded paint-brush as it streaks across familiar scenes, illuminating them from within. His subject matter was typically dictated by his patrons – biblical scenes, mythical allegories, odes to the greats of Venice – but he made them seem new with his careful spotlighting, stormy backdrops and vertigo-inducing perspective.

A crash course in Tintoretto begins at his preserved *bottega* (workshop; p81), then nips around the corner to Chiesa della Madonna dell'Orto (p74), his parish church and the serene backdrop for his action-packed 1546 *Last Judgment*. True-blue Venetian that he is, Tintoretto shows the final purge as a teal tidal wave, with lost souls vainly trying to hold it back like human MOSE barriers (see p172). The riveting image of a dive-bombing angel swooping in to save one last person was reprised by Tintoretto in the upper floor of Scuola Grande di San Rocco (pictured above; p86), where he spent some 15 years creating works for the patron saint of plague victims. His biblical scenes here read like a graphic novel, with backdrops fading to black to capture the drama of Jesus' final days and the Black Death, the darkness lightened only by the artist's streaky white rays of hope.

>5 TITIAN

TRAIL TITIAN ACROSS TOWN FROM MASTERPIECE TO MASTERPIECE

In other cities you might actually have to search to find artistic inspiration, but in Venice you can just follow the footbridges to the first, last, and best paintings by the master of the red-hot moment. At the Santa Maria della Salute (p112), you'll notice Titian started out a measured, methodical painter in his 1510 *St Marco Enthroned*, although his brushwork was already loose enough and vermillion vibrant enough to add dynamism to a straightforward scene. But after seeing Michelangelo's writhing *Last Judgment* Titian let it rip, and his expressive urgency is palpable in his final 1576 *Pietà*, where he smeared paint onto the canvas with his bare hands.

But even for a man of many masterpieces, Titian's *Madonna of the Assumption* at I Frari (pictured above; p84) is an astonishing accomplishment. Titian has captured the instant when the Madonna has risen beyond the grasp of the lowly mortals below, with the angels putting their backs into the final push. This altarpiece seems to fill the nave with the radiant warmth of the Madonna's red robes, and that pale wrist revealed by a slipping sleeve has been known to get priests too hot and bothered to pray.

>6 LA BIENNALE DI VENEZIA

GLIMPSE THE FUTURE AT LA BIENNALE DI VENEZIA

Seems like every dreary German city holds a contemporary-art biennale these days – but when connoisseurs talk about *the* Biennale, they still mean Venice. Started in 1895 to provide an essential corrective to the brutality of the Industrial Revolution and to reassert Venice's role as global tastemaker, the Biennale was initially a conservative institution. A grand garden pavilion provided a studiously inoffensive take on Italy's latest artistic achievements – principally lovely ladies, pretty flowers and lovely ladies wearing pretty flowers. Other nations were granted pavilions in 1907, but the Biennale foundation still retained strict control, even removing a Picasso from the Spanish Pavilion in 1910 so as not to shock the public with modernity.

Then one world war after another erupted, making such delicacy seem terribly antiquated. The post-WWI Biennale boldly exhibited works by Amedeo Modigliani, whose abstract blank-eyed women were hotly debated. Venice wasn't instantly convinced by modernism, but it did discover an appetite for artistic controversy, as new pavilions for Korea, Japan and Canada highlighted avant-garde art and architecture. While many Venetians mock the Biennale's rather pretentious recent motto *Pensa con i Sensi/Senti con la Mente* (Think with the Senses/Feel with the Mind), the Biennale's autumn showcases for avant-garde architecture (in even-numbered years) and art (odd-numbered years) are eagerly anticipated.

See p29 and p59 for more.

>7 VENICE FILM FESTIVAL

WATCH THE STARS ALIGN AT THE VENICE FILM FESTIVAL

When the Venice Biennale announced its first film showcase in 1932, the scandal threatened to sink Venice. 'What kind of a city would risk its reputation on popular entertainment?' sniffed Cannes, New York and Telluride. The Oscars were still being held in the Fiesta Room at Hollywood's Ambassador Hotel (seating capacity: 900), so no one imagined that the far-flung Lido would be swamped with filmgoers. But once Joan Crawford and Clark Gable hit the red carpet, and 25,000 people showed up for screenings, the festival and its Golden Lion awards proved to be a winning formula of art and celebrity.

Never an indie-film showcase, the Venice Film Festival has gained a reputation as the film festival that rewards directors who should have won Oscars on sheer creative merit. Directors featured at Venice include David Fincher (*Fight Club*), Spike Jonze (*Being John Malkovich*), Antoine Fuqua (*Training Day*) and Ang Lee (*Brokeback Mountain*), as well as perennial favourites Woody Allen, Takeshi Kitano, Martin Scorsese and Zhang Yimou.

See p29 and p135 for more.

> 8 THE GHETTO

EXPLORE THE GHETTO, THE NEIGHBOURHOOD THAT LAUNCHED A RENAISSANCE

Standing in the Ghetto's lopsided main square (p71), surrounded by ramshackle buildings, you'd never guess that this was the heart of an empire. In accordance with the Venetian Republic's 1516 decree, by day Jewish lenders funded Venice's commercial enterprises, while by night and on Christian holidays they were restricted to the gated Ghetto Nuovo.

When Jewish merchants fled to Venice from the Spanish Inquisition in 1541, there was no place for them to go but up. Additional storeys on existing buildings in the Ghetto housed new arrivals and synagogues, while across town the Renaissance was advanced by Jewish lenders and Jewish artisans, filling palaces and churches with priceless treasures. But through papal restrictions and plague, the Ghetto was reduced to 3000 inhabitants by 1670.

After Napoleon lifted restrictions in 1797, Ghetto residents gained standing as Venetian citizens. But Mussolini's 1938 race laws were throwbacks to the 16th century, and in 1943 most of the 1670 Jews in Venice were rounded up and sent to concentration camps; only 37 returned. Venice's Jewish community now numbers around 420, but children playing tag in the *campo* (square) show there's still life left in the Ghetto. To explore some of the Ghetto's seven synagogues (pictured above), book a tour with the Museo Ebraico di Venezia (p75).

>9 NIGHT AT THE OPERA

GET A PERFORMANCE HIGH AT TEATRO LA FENICE

No matter what's on the bill at Teatro La Fenice (p57), there's bound to be drama. Before the doors open, the buzz begins at cafes around the piazza, where tousled artistes and coiffed socialites gather to toss back prosecco with an espresso chaser. Once the crowd heads inside the theatre, wraps are shed in lower-tier boxes to reveal jewels and Murano-glass baubles, while in the cheap seats of the top-tier *loggie* (balconies), the *loggione* (opera critics) predict which singers will be in good voice and which understudies may be due for a promotion. Architecture aficionados find other subjects to argue about – namely whether the historically accurate reconstruction after the 1996 fire was worth €90 million, or whether the baroque 'inverted-wedding-cake' style should have been modernised by architect Gae Aulenti as originally planned. But when the overture begins, all voices hush and the air turns electric with anticipation. No one wants to miss a note of a performance that could compare with historic premieres by Stravinsky, Rossini, Prokofiev, Britten and, of course, Giuseppe Verdi.

>10 BEHIND THE SCENES

VEER OFF THE TOURIST TRACK TO HIDDEN GEMS

Pity the cruise-ship crowds dropped off at San Marco with a mere two hours to take in Venice. That's about enough time for one long gasp at the show-stopper that is Piazza San Marco, but not nearly enough to see what else Venice is hiding behind its Moorish Gothic portals. For those who stray off the tourist trail, yellow signs helpfully point the way back to San Marco from the obvious landmarks of the Rialto, Gallerie dell'Accademia and train station, bypassing a maze of *calli* (streets), *sotoportegi* (passageways) and canals. But here's the secret to any great Venetian adventure: *ignore those signs.*

With an adventurous spirit and a decent map, you can plunge into Venice's labyrinth, discovering the city behind the Grand Canal facades. Dine like a local in hidden *cortili* (courtyards), stay overnight in a *palazzo* (palace or mansion) and wake up to the sound of gondolieri calling 'Ooooooeeeeeee!' as they manoeuvre long boats around blind corners. From where you stand at a local *bacaro* (bar), you can watch the day trippers thunder past to their trains, planes and buses, and simply drink in Venice.

>11 CA' REZZONICO

SEE HOW VENICE'S SPIRITS SOARED, EVEN AS ITS POWER WANED, AT CA' REZZONICO

Saying that Venice's glory days ended with the 16th century is like saying the city peaked while a teenager – and it completely overlooks the splendours of Ca' Rezzonico, aka the Museum of 18th-Century Venice.

For all its breezy gorgeousness, the Ca' Rezzonico's wits are razor sharp. Airy and light without seeming frou-frou, the Ca' Rezzonico is a Baldassare Longhena–designed palace that was just right for its time. Giambattista Tiepolo covered the Ca' Rezzonico's ceilings with shamelessly flattering paintings, showing Ludovico Rezzonico and his bride surrounded by Fame, Wisdom and Merit – but these trompe l'œil domes are so clever, colourful and overtly theatrical that it seems Tiepolo was just gleefully showing off.

By the 18th century, Venice had lived through plague, defended itself against Turkish invasion and seen its world-domination ambitions dashed – but it was determined to make light of a dire situation, and its tragicomic tendencies are captured in the art of the period. An entire drawing room at the Ca' Rezzonico is dedicated to Pietro Longhi's drawing-room satires, including *The Morning Chocolate* (1775), which shows fashionable Venetians bingeing on trendy cocoa and doughnuts at the risk of popping their waistcoat buttons or upsetting a disapproving lapdog. Rosalba Carriera captures her sitters' every quirk in her pastel portraits, and their sly smirks make them look like the life of any 18th-century party.

See p109 for more information.

>12 GOING FOR BAROQUE

HEAR BAROQUE LIKE NEVER BEFORE

When pop seems overplayed and jazz standards a little too standard, Venice offers an alternative: baroque. Venetian baroque was the rebel music of its day, openly defying edicts from Rome that set down which instruments could accompany sermons, and what kinds of rhythms and melodies were suitable for uplifting morals. But Venetians kept on playing stringed instruments in churches, singing along to bawdy *opera buffa* (comic opera), and capturing the full range of human experience in sensual, explosive compositions. Modern misconceptions that baroque is simply a nice accompaniment to wedding ceremonies are smashed by baroque 'early-music' ensembles such as Venice Baroque Opera, which commands international followings with its original 18th-century instruments and shockingly contemporary interpretations of baroque pieces.

Venice's best-loved composer is Vivaldi, and though his *Four Seasons* may be instantly recognisable from hotel-lobby muzak and mobile-phone ringtones, you haven't really heard summer lightning strike and spring threaten to flood the room until you've heard Vivaldi played by Interpreti Veneziani (p97). Also look for programs featuring Venetian baroque composer Tomaso Albinoni.

Finally, make sure you consider the venue – any baroque performance in the Casa di Goldoni (p84), the Ca' Rezzonico (p109) or the Ospedaletto (pictured above; p63) will transport you to the 18th century in one movement, and catapult you into the 21st in the next.

>13 TORCELLO & BURANO

EXPLORE THE OUTER LIMITS OF THE LAGOON ON TORCELLO AND BURANO

Once you've wrapped your head around the improbable existence of Venice – who builds a city on a silty lagoon? – Burano (p140) and Torcello (p144) defy your imagination all over again.

Photographers in inspiration overdrive dash off the ferry into Burano's backstreets, snapping away at turquoise window boxes filled with red geraniums, and green stockings hung out to dry between pink and orange houses. Either there is some law requiring locals to choose contrasting paint schemes and complementary-colour skivvies, or Burano is naturally the most artistically inclined fishing village in the Mediterranean basin.

On the pastoral island of Torcello, sheep easily outnumber the 20 or so human residents. But this bucolic backwater was once a Byzantine metropolis of 20,000 – and it has the stunning mosaics to prove it. In a scene from the Last Judgment in Torcello's Cattedrale di Santa Maria Assunta, a band of holy avengers arrives to save the day: Jesus breaks down the doors of hell while a sea nymph representing the Adriatic ushers souls lost at sea towards Peter, who's jangling the keys to Paradise like God's own bouncer. These Byzantine mosaics are often compared to those in the Basilica di San Marco but, if you want an epic adventure, Torcello is worth the trip.

>14 DUCAL PALACE

TAKE A WALK TO THE DOGI'S DARK SIDE IN THE DUCAL PALACE

From the outside, the restored Ducal Palace is all elegant brickwork and graceful Gothic colonnades, but the inside of the *palazzo* reveals a darker side to the dogi (Venice's leaders). Right behind a grand salon festooned with cherubim and Paolo Veronese's allegories of Virtue conquering Vice lie the cramped secret headquarters of the shadowy Consiglio dei Dieci (Council of Ten), Venice's version of the CIA. Upstairs was the Piombi, the dread attic prison where Casanova was sentenced to five years' confinement on charges of corrupting nuns and spreading Freemasonry.

Casanova charmed his way past the guards in 1757, and you too can plot your escape from the Piombi on the fascinating Itinerari Segreti (Secret Passageways) tour. This tour leads you through the Consiglio dei Dieci's administrative offices to a windowless room with a single rope: the dogi's torture chamber. To Venice's credit, the room was largely disused by the 17th century – but the same cannot be said for the studded cells where the accused awaited trial. Renaissance Venice was no place for rebels: anyone who dared question the rosy depiction of Venetian government on view downstairs just might be taken upstairs.

See p45 for more information.

>15 PALAZZO GRASSI

EXPERIENCE THE SHOCK OF THE NEW AT PALAZZO GRASSI

Paris is still burning with indignation over the decision by French billionaire François Pinault to showcase his vast art collection in a Venetian *palazzo*. In 2006, Pinault bought the Grassi (p47) from the Fiat Group, hiring celebrated minimalist architect Tadao Ando to update the palace to accommodate both Pinault's personal contemporary-art collection and ambitious reappraisals of art history, such as the recent *Rome and the Barbarians* show. The results are simply startling. Ando's stark partitions are capped with perfect halos of lighting, illuminating a past worth reconsidering and a future worth turning the next corner to find.

But the spectacular exhibition space and the clever curation are only part of the attraction. Facing the Grand Canal, the Grassi uses its pier for sculpture installations, surprising gondola riders with Jeff Koons' shiny magenta *Balloon Dog*, and Subodh Gupta's *Very Hungry God*, a gigantic skull made entirely of aluminium cookware. The 1st-floor cafe is actually an art installation that serves espresso; its conceptual decor is reinvented for each show by a contemporary artist to reflect that show's theme.

Until Pinault and Ando's next project, the Punta della Dogana (p114), opens in 2009, the Grassi remains the hottest art ticket in town.

>VENICE DIARY

Three rules for revellers are posted at vaporetto (city-ferry) stops: no littering in the canals, no defacing historic buildings and no strutting about bare breasted. The fact that Venice feels obliged to post that last regulation shows that opportunities for, erm, self-expression don't begin and end with Carnevale. Whether you like to spend your downtime getting arty, sweaty, mystical or all of the above, Venice has you covered, with Biennales, marathons and weddings to the sea. A warning, though: this town seems determined to see you dunked. Many festivals entail crossing makeshift pontoon bridges or rowing while standing up – and boozing canalside has obvious risks.

Portrait of a lady: Carnevale (p28) is the perfect time to discover your inner paparazzo

VENICE DIARY

FEBRUARY

Carnevale

www.carnevale.venezia.it

Even Napoleon couldn't stop Venice's signature event. Before Lent begins, masqueraders party in the streets – and occasionally fall into canals – in long-nosed masks and commedia dell'arte costumes. If your liver hurts and wig itches after 10 days, just imagine how you'd have felt in the 18th century, when the party lasted up to three months.

APRIL

Festa di San Marco

www.comune.venezia.it

Citizen Kane would appreciate the celebration of Venice's patron saint on 25 April – the recurring motif is a *bocolo* (rosebud). Venetian men carry roses in processions through Piazza San Marco, and give them to the women they love best.

Scare small children during Carnevale

TOP FIVE WAYS TO CELEBRATE CARNEVALE

> Slide tackle in knee britches at Calcio Storico, a fancy-dress football match in Piazza San Marco.
> Binge on *frittelle*, the rum-raisin doughnuts that are best eaten when still warm.
> Quadrille the night away at Teatro La Fenice's masked ball on the second Saturday of Carnevale (tickets start at €200; costume and dance classes not included).
> Watch the Grand Canal parade, where the floats actually float.
> Have a historically accurate blast, or DIY trying, by making your own costume and mastering the art of mask acting at Teatro Junghans (p131).

MAY

Vogalonga

www.turismovenezia.it

Not so much a race as a test of endurance, this 32km 'Long Row' starts with 1000 boats in front of the Ducal Palace, loops past Burano and Murano, and ends several boats shy of the starting number at Punta della Dogana.

Festa della Sensa

www.sevenonline.it/sensa

Venice loves its lagoon so much that it has renewed its vows to the water every year since AD 998. In the Sposalizio del Mar (Wedding to the Sea), the mayor tosses a gold ring in the waters near San Nicolò on the Lido.

JUNE

Venezia Suona

www.veneziasuona.it

Hear medieval *campi* (squares) and baroque *palazzi* (palaces or mansions) echo with the latest sounds from around the world.

La Biennale di Venezia

www.labiennale.org

In odd-numbered years the Art Biennale usually runs from June to November, and in even years the Architecture Biennale kicks off in September – but every summer there's also avant-garde dance, theatre, cinema and music. See p17.

JULY

Festa del Rendentore

www.turismovenezia.it

Walk on water across the Canal della Giudecca to Il Redentore (p128) via a wobbly pontoon bridge on the third Saturday and Sunday in July. Join the floating picnic along the Zattere, and don't miss the fireworks.

AUGUST

Venice Film Festival

www.labiennale.org/en/cinema

The only thing hotter than Lido beaches in August is the red carpet at this star-studded event, which runs from the last weekend in August through the first week of September.

Star-gaze at the Venice Film Festival

SEPTEMBER

Venice Video Art Fair
www.venicevideoartfair.org
Often poetic, pretty and quite weird all at once, Italy's premier video-art fair features 25 booths of new-media art in the anachronistic island setting of San Servolo, located a ferry ride away from the Biennale Internazionale d'Arte pavilions.

Regata Storica
www.comune.venezia.it
Never mind who's winning, check out all the cool gear. At the Historical Regatta, 16th-century costumes, eight-oared gondolas and

ceremonial barques all feature in a procession reenacting the arrival of the queen of Cyprus. Kids, women and gondolieri compete for boating bragging rights.

Regata di Burano
www.comune.venezia.it
The final grudge match of the regatta season, the Regata di Burano is the race where rowers either gloat over their definitive win or take consolation in plenty of local fish, polenta and white wine.

OCTOBER

Venice Marathon
www.venicemarathon.com
Six thousand runners work up a sweat over 42km of spectacular scenery, dashing along the River Brenta past Palladian villas before crossing into Venice and heading to Piazza San Marco via a 160m floating bridge. Mind your step...

NOVEMBER

Festa della Madonna della Salute
www.turismovenezia.it
If you'd survived plague and Austrian invasion, you'd throw a party too. Every 21 November since the 17th century, Venetians have crossed a pontoon bridge across the Grand Canal to give thanks at Chiesa di Santa Maria della Salute (p112) and splurge on sweets.

Watch rowers make history at the Regata Storica

Every dog has its day in the piazzas of Venice

ITINERARIES

Why bother with time machines? A walk across Venice takes you from golden Byzantium to the Titian red Renaissance, from Vivaldi to video art. Immerse yourself in Venice's historical splendours, then step into the future with musical performances, contemporary art and artisanal handicrafts.

DAY ONE

Begin your day in prison on the Itinerari Segreti (Secret Passageways) tour of the Ducal Palace (p45), then make a break for Piazza San Marco. Lunch at Cava Tappi (p53) will get you ready to take on the Gallerie dell'Accademia (p113), after which it's time for *aperitivi* and people-watching in Campo Santa Margherita. Grab a bite at Osteria alla Bifora (p123) before your Interpreti Veneziani concert (p97), held among Tin-toretto masterpieces at Scuola Grande di San Rocco (p86). End the night gliding down the Grand Canal on a vaporetto (city ferry) or gondola.

DAY TWO

The Basilica di San Marco (p41) starts your day with a dazzle, and the art attack continues with modern art at Palazzo Grassi (p47), and Tintorettos and Canovas at Santo Stefano (p48). Your growling stomach will lead you across the Rialto to All'Arco (p91) for Francesco and Matteo's latest *cicheti* (Venetian tapas) creations, and to Gelateria San Stae (p105) for an ice cream. Make a cameo appearance in the costume drama of the museum of textiles at Palazzo Mocenigo (p102), then get lost in the former red-light district near Ponte delle Tette (p85) en route to Titian's masterpiece at I Frari (p84). Dine at Enoteca ai Artisti (p119), but chase that amarone with an espresso – tonight's entertainment is a performance at Teatro La Fenice (p57).

DAY THREE

Andrea Palladio's white Chiesa di San Giorgio Maggiore (p126) is beauti-fully blinding as you approach by vaporetto. Check out the Tintorettos by the altar, then nip around the back to see contemporary art at Fondazione Giorgio Cini (p127). Catch another vaporetto to lunch at I Figli delle Stelle

Top left Get your daily exercise while exploring Venice's hidden bridges and passageways **Top right** Sigh over the stunning Ponte dei Sospiri (p45) **Bottom** Cruisin' down the river: classic Venetian transport, classic Venetian view

(p130), then gallery-hop your way to Il Redentore (p128) and Fortuny Tessuti Artistici (p128). Ride the vaporetto to Zattere for ice cream at Da Nico (p119) and wall-to-wall Paolo Veronese paintings in Chiesa di San Sebastiano (p109). Pay your respects to Peggy Guggenheim (p113), then head back to San Marco for dinner at Aciugheta (p66), jailhouse jazz by Jazz in Venice (p69), and a toast to San Marco at Aurora Caffè (p56).

RAINY DAY

Skip the long, wet lines at the Gallerie dell'Accademia and Basilica di San Marco, and head to I Frari (p84) to bask in the glow of Titian's *Madonna of the Assumption*. Duck into the Scuola Grande di San Rocco (p86), where Tintoretto's stormy canvases make Venetian weather seem balmy, then warm up afterwards with prosecco and polenta at ImprontaCafé (p119). At the nearby Scuola Grande dei Carmini (p114), pass cloudy grey paintings downstairs and head up Baldassare Longhena's stairway to heaven to find the silver lining: Giambattista Tiepolo's *Virtues* ceiling. Blue skies are ahead at Ca' Rezzonico (p109), where Tiepolo's trompe l'œil sunlight brightens salon ceilings. Afterwards, pasta at Ristoteca Oniga (p120) will warm you from the inside out.

It might be *alta acqua* (high water) in Piazza San Marco (p40), but at least you can say you walked on water

FORWARD PLANNING

Three weeks before you go Book tickets online for opera at Teatro La Fenice (p57), movie premieres at the Venice Film Festival (p29) and the Itinerari Segreti (Secret Passageways) tour of the Ducal Palace (p45).

One week before you go Get your ticket online to the Art or Architecture Biennale (p29), call ahead for tickets to see Interpreti Veneziani (p97) in concert at the splendid Scuola Grande di San Rocco, and skip the queues by booking tickets to the Gallerie dell'Accademia (p113) and various concerts at http://en.venezia.waf.it.

One day before you go Find out what live music, art openings and festivals are happening tomorrow in Venice at www.venezianews.it, www.veneziadavivere.com and www.aguestin-venice.com; call to reserve a spot on Museo Ebraico di Venezia's tour (p75) of three to five of the historic synagogues in the Ghetto; call to book a restaurant for tomorrow; and pack your umbrella, swimsuit and powdered wig to cover all Venetian possibilities.

BEACH DAY

Hop on a vaporetto to the Lido and loll the day away on a beach chair, watching celebrities and ships drift past. Restless types can rent a bike at Lido on Bike (p136) and pedal 1.5km north towards the Antico Cimitero Israelitico (p134), or cruise 6km down pine-shaded beachfront to the canal-lined town of Malamocco (p135). Unwind with happy-hour cocktails at the Colony Bar (p136), set on the verandah of historic Hotel des Bains, then grab dinner in the breezy garden at Trattoria La Favorita (p136). At night, catch a movie at the Venice Film Festival (p29) or Multi-sala Astra (p137), live music at Aurora Beach Club (p137), or beach DJ sets at Ultima Spiaggia di Pachuka (p137).

ON THE CHEAP

Wander past pavilions representing countless architectural styles in the gardens of the Biennale Internazionale d'Arte (p59), from the secession-ist Austro-Hungarian Pavilion to the postindustrial Korea Pavilion. Stroll up the boardwalk to Basilica di San Marco (p41) to see priceless mosaics, gratis. Window-shop your way to the Rialto produce markets (p94) for fresh food and maybe even a free sample, then have a picnic at Campo San Gia-cometto. Head back across the Rialto to the Ghetto (p19) to spot rooftop synagogues and reflect on Venice's Jewish history before heading to Osteria agli Ormesini (p80) to see who'll buy you a drink. In summer, check out Campo San Polo (p97) for free outdoor music, movies and theatre.

Postcard perfect: the Ponte di Rialto (p86) is simply stunning

SESTIERI

For a city of islands, Venice isn't especially insular. Historically many Venetians rarely left their *sestieri* (neighbourhoods), and some were loath to even leave the island where they lived – but there's a certain logic to that inertia. Why would they need to leave when the world would come to them?

When Venetians such as Marco Polo did shove off from these shores, they returned with stories, ideas and booty from countries as far away as Mongolia. Even after its glory days as a global trading hub passed, Venice continued to attract poets, bon vivants and billionaire art collectors – anyone for whom beauty trumped convenience.

Even though it's now more accessible than ever, Venice remains a self-selecting city: only art and films that have proven themselves elsewhere make it to the Venice Biennale and the Venice Film Festival. But that doesn't make it snobby. The city welcomes anyone who manages to find their way to the outer reaches of Cannaregio, Castello, Santa Croce or Giudecca, or sticks around San Marco after the sightseers have cleared out.

Island fever isn't really a problem here. The *sestieri* are different enough that when restlessness begins to set in, you can just cross a couple of bridges or hop on a vaporetto (city ferry) to get a fresh perspective on the city. Overwhelmed by Byzantine glitz, Bellinis and shoe shopping in San Marco? Head to Santa Croce, where baroque edifices shelter modest cafes, wine comes straight from the cask, and talk revolves around boats and Berlusconi. For a change of pace from the industrial cool of Giudecca, wander across to Castello, where a stretch of greenery awaits you. If you hit church overload in San Polo, you might explore synagogues in Cannaregio instead. When Lido beaches get crowded with fashionistas in giant hats, Dorsoduro's Zattere waterfront offers sun without the scene. To get away from it all, head for open waters and remote islands on the lagoon. It's all Venice, and it's all good.

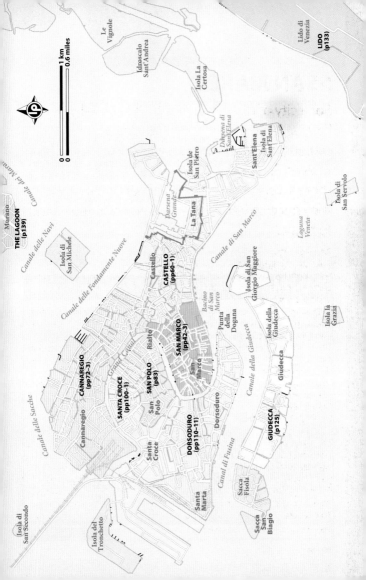

THE LAGOON (p139)

Murano

LIDO
Lido di
Venezia

LIDO (p133)

Le
Vignole

Idroscalo
Sant'Andrea

Isola La
Certosa

Isola di
San Servolo

Canale dei Marani

Canale delle Navi

Isola di
San Michele

Canale delle Fondamente Nuove

Darsena di
Sant'Elena

Sant'Elena
Isola di
Sant'Elena

Isola de
San Pietro

Dàrsena
Grande

La Tana

CASTELLO
(pp60–1)

Castello

Canale di San Marco

Laguna
Veneta

CANNAREGIO
(pp72–3)

Rialto

Grand Canal

SAN MARCO
(pp42–3)

Bacino
di San
Marco

Isola di San
Giorgio Maggiore

Isola la
Grazia

Cannaregio

SANTA CROCE
(pp100–1)

SAN POLO
(p83)

San
Polo

San
Marco

Punta
della
Dogana

Santa
Croce

DORSODURO
(pp110–11)

Dorsoduro

Isola della
Giudecca

Canale della Giudecca

Isola di
San Secondo

Santa
Marta

Canal di Fusina

Sacca
Fisola

GIUDECCA
(p125)

Giudecca

Isola del
Tronchetto

Sacca
San
Biagio

Canale delle Sacche

1 km
0.6 miles

>SAN MARCO

So many world-renowned attractions are packed into San Marco that
some visitors never leave – while others are loath to visit, fearing a crush
of day trippers and unappetising tourist menus. But it would be unfair to
dismiss San Marco simply as a tourist trap. Piazza San Marco is gorgeously
deserted by sunset, and just down San Marco's backstreets are authentic
osterie (restaurant-bars) where you can eat and drink like a local. Besides,
why deny yourself the pleasure of Teatro La Fenice, Basilica di San Marco,
Palazzo Grassi and the Ducal Palace just to be contrarian? Go and judge
for yourself whether these cultural landmarks earn their world-class reputations – but don't stop there. San Marco is packed with contemporary
art galleries, chic boutiques and trendy *bacari* (bars). Rather than rest on
its considerable laurels, San Marco keeps the inspiration coming.

SAN MARCO

👁 SEE

🛍 SHOP

🍴 EAT

🍷 DRINK

⭐ PLAY

Please see over for map

◐ SEE

◐ BASILICA DI SAN MARCO

☎ 041 5225205; www.basilicasanmarco
.it; Piazza San Marco; basilica free, Pala
d'Oro/Loggia dei Cavalli & Museum/
Treasury €2/3/2; ⏱ 9.45am-5pm
Mon-Sat, 2-4pm Sun & holidays; 🚊 San
Marco, San Zaccaria, Vallaresso

If seen-it-all modern visitors gasp
to discover bright-eyed apostles
and luminous angels staring down
from San Marco's golden domes,
just imagine visitors' reactions in
the Middle Ages. At the time, most
medieval buildings in the region
were low wooden structures,
indoor lighting was dim and colour
pigments were rare imported

luxuries – and here was a soaring
stone structure with sunlight
bouncing off millions of tiny
tesserae made from gold and
crushed semiprecious stones.
Since San Marco was officially
the chapel of the doge (Venice's
leader), the dogi took to displaying
stolen treasures in the basilica, including the gilded bronze
horses from Constantinople that
high-stepped over the central
portal. (These were later stolen by
Napoleon, but are now on display
inside; the ones over the portal on
the Loggia dei Cavalli are copies.)
Church authorities in Rome took a
dim view of Venice's tendency to
glorify itself and God in the same

Get a horse's-eye view of the piazza from the Basilica di San Marco

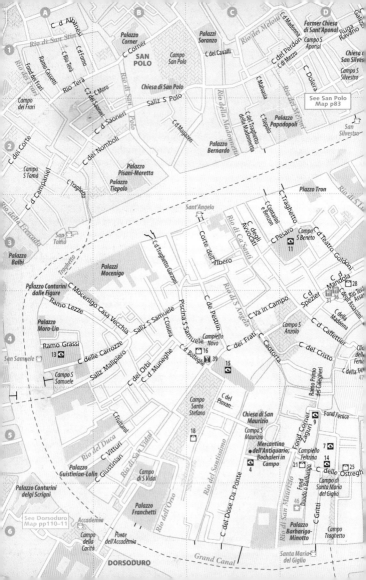

SESTIERI

SAN MARCO

breath, but Venice finished San Marco as it saw fit: the basilica's grand East-meets-West cosmopolitan style includes Eastern onion-bulb domes, a Greek cross layout, Gothic arches, and dizzying puzzle-work floors made from Egyptian marble. The roped-off circuit of the church is free and takes about 15 minutes; going through twice is recommended to recover from the initial astonishment. The Loggia dei Cavalli is worth a look for its views over Piazza San Marco, but the alabaster chalices and icons in the Treasury can't quite compare to the exquisite enamel miniatures on the bejewelled Pala d'Oro altarpiece. Note that you'll need to be dressed modestly (ie knees and shoulders covered) to enter the basilica, and large bags must be left around the corner at **Ateneo di San Basso** (☽ 9.30am-5.30pm). See p10 for more information.

☉ CAMPANILE DI SAN MARCO
☎ 041 5225205; www.basilicasanmarco .it; Piazza San Marco; admission €8; ☽ 9am-7pm Apr-Jun & Oct, 9am-9pm Jul-Sep, 9.30am-3.45pm Nov-Mar; 🚊 San Marco, Vallaresso
There's no such thing as tall enough or skinny enough for this bell tower's critics, who for centuries have called the 99m brick tower squat and ungainly. But when the tower – which was raised in AD 888 and rebuilt in 1514 –

unexpectedly collapsed in a heap in 1902, city leaders rebuilt it exactly as it was. Fondness for the icon that served as the city's lighthouse trumped the objections of naysayers, who have to concede that the view from the top is breathtaking.

☉ CATERINA TOGNON ARTE
☎ 041 5207859; www.caterinatognon .com; Campo San Maurizio 2671; admission free; ☽ 3-7pm Mon-Sat; 🚊 Santa Maria del Giglio
Don't be fooled by the small storefront space: Tognon makes a big splash, with a spirited mix of emerging and established contemporary artists both here and at the adjacent stART space (entrance through Tognon) in 17th-century Palazzo da Ponte. A major recent show of avant-garde glassworks featured Kiki Smith's visceral vessels and Roberta Silva's single exhalation captured for poetic posterity in a glass bubble.

☉ CLOCK TOWER
☎ 041 5209070; www.museicivicivenez iani.it; Piazza San Marco; tour €12, with VeniceCard €7; ☽ tours 10am, 11am & 1pm Mon-Wed, 2pm, 3pm & 5pm Thu-Sun; 🚊 San Marco, Vallaresso
Legend has it that the experts who invented the works of this astro-nomical clock were assassinated so that no other city could boast a similar engineering marvel. But

now visitors can see for themselves what makes this tower tick on special tours of the recently renovated monument. The terrace looks past the statues of the two Moors over Piazza San Marco, and the view is well worth the climb up the steep, claustrophobia-triggering spiral staircase. In the piazza, look up to see three kings and an angel emerge from the clock on Epiphany (6 January) and the Feast of the Ascension (second Sunday in May).

◉ DUCAL PALACE

☎ 041 2715911; www.museiciviciveneziani.it; Piazza San Marco 52; adult/student incl Museo Correr & 1 civic museum €13/8; ⏰ 9am-7pm Apr-Oct, 9am-5pm Nov-Mar; 🚊 San Marco, Vallaresso

All the show-stopping splendour and sinister intrigue of the Venetian Republic are captured in this one civic monument, which is best viewed on the riveting **Itinerari Segreti** (Secret Passageways; tour incl admission to Ducal Palace €16; ⏰ tours 9.55am, 10.45am & 11.35am) tour.

Enter through the Gothic-colonnaded courtyard, climb the Scala dei Censori (Stairs of the Censors) and Sansovino's Scala d'Oro (Golden Staircase), and emerge into rooms covered with gorgeous propaganda: Tintoretto's depictions of Venice's virtues, Giambattista Tiepolo's *Venice Receiving the Gifts of the Sea from Neptune* and, finally, the Council Room

designe... Paolo V... tering ... governm... trial cha... dei Diec... dreaded... the slot where written denunciations were placed, as well as Veronese's paintings of Juno scattering her gifts on Venice. Behind the doge's throne in the cavernous Grand Council room (inaugurated in 1419) is a vision of Paradise by Tintoretto's son Domenico that's more politically correct than pretty, crammed with 500 portraits of prominent Venetians (and Tintoretto patrons). Downstairs are hellish scenes by the master of apocalyptic visions, Hieronymus Bosch. Across the Ponte dei Sospiri (Bridge of Sighs) are Venice's 16th-century Prigione Nuove (New Prisons), dank cells covered with graffiti and protestations of innocence. Emerge from the dark side of Venice into the sunlight, and admire the pinkish palace loggia graced with lacy 15th-century Gothic arches. See p25 for more.

◉ GALLERIA TRAGHETTO

☎ 041 5221188; www.galleriatraghetto.it, in Italian; Campo Santa Maria del Giglio 2543; admission free; ⏰ 3-7pm Mon-Sat; 🚊 Santa Maria del Giglio

This gallery has gutsy shows of young Italian and international

...he brink of break-
... Look for Rome-based Ser-
... Maiorano's artfully blurred
...gital photographs, with bleeding
reds that evoke the work of Vittore Carpaccio, and paintings by
Lithuanian Andrius Zakarauskas,
where history is cleverly reduced
to saluting, finger pointing and
other iconic gestures.

◉ JARACH GALLERY

☎ 041 5221938; www.jarachgallery
.com; Campo San Fantin 1997; admission
free; ⏲ 2-8pm Tue-Sun; ⚓ Santa Maria
del Giglio

While diva Teatro La Fenice holds
centre stage in this piazza, this
contemporary-photography
gallery waits in the wings. Both
the gallery's location – through a
shadowy *sotoportego* (passageway) – and program are big on
quiet drama and mystery; Giorgio
Barrera, for example, staged
crimes that were glimpsed, while
in progress, through Venetian
Gothic windows.

◉ LA GALLERIA VAN DER KOELEN

☎ 041 5207415; www.galerie.vander
koelen.de; Ramo Primo dei Calegheri
2566; admission free; ⏲ 10am-12.30pm
& 3.30-6.30pm Mon-Sat; ⚓ Santa Maria
del Giglio

Keeping a low profile behind
the loud, proud La Fenice, and

contrasting with the onslaught
of colour and drama that is the
Gallerie dell'Accademia, La Galleria is the eye in the centre of
Venice's aesthetic storm. A recent
show featured Günther Uecker's
delicately brutal embossed-paper
nails and detailed drawings of
glass shards.

◉ MUSEO CORRER

☎ 041 2405211; www.museicivicivenez
iani.it; Piazza San Marco 52; adult/stu-
dent incl Ducal Palace & 1 civic museum
€13/8; ⏲ 9am-7pm Apr-Oct, 9am-5pm
Nov-Mar; ⚓ San Marco, Vallaresso

Snicker if you must at his oversized
hats and undersized beds, but
Napoleon knew something about
organisation, both military and architectural. Never mind that there
was a church on the west end
of Piazza San Marco: Napoleon
razed the place to make room
for a grand ballroom. Today the
Museo Correr unifies the 1st and
2nd floors of the arcade overlooking the piazza, leading through
Graeco-Roman statuary and
splendid medieval paintings, and
culminating in Venice's crown-
ing glory: the Libreria Nazionale
Marciana's 16th-century reading
room, with representations of wisdom by Veronese and Titian. Don't
miss the Caffè dell'Arte, covered
in baroque grotesques of griffins
and other beasties, and ideal for a
€4 glass of Veneto merlot served

with views of San Marco worthy of an emperor.

MUSEO FORTUNY

☎ 041 5209070; www.museicivicivenez iani.it; Campo San Beneto 3958; admission €8, with VeniceCard €5; ☼ 10am-6pm Wed-Mon; ☷ Sant'Angelo

An eccentric for the ages and truly avant-garde, Spanish designer Mariano Fortuny y Madrazo loosened Victorian corsets with free-flowing Grecian dresses that drew bohemian devotees such as Isadora Duncan to his Gothic showroom. The rotating exhibitions are of variable interest, but the permanent draws are Moorish-deco chandeliers, salons sumptuously swagged with Fortuny's printed silks, and the top-floor workshop with design sketches from 1910 that still look modern.

PALAZZO CONTARINI DEL BOVOLO

☎ 041 5322920; Calle Contarini del Bovolo 4299; courtyard free; ☼ 10am-6pm; ☷ Rialto

Never mind that you can't peek inside the 15th-century *palazzo* (palace or mansion), or that the *bovolo* (snail-shell) staircase, wrapped in brick and decorated with white cutaway archways, is closed for restoration – the courtyard offers the best view of this jewel of Renaissance architecture.

PALAZZO GRASSI

☎ 041 5231680; www.palazzograssi.it; Campo San Samuele 3231; adult/student €15/6; ☼ 10am-7pm; ☷ San Samuele

Anachronism has never looked as glorious as it does in Giorgio Masari's 1749 neoclassical palace, with its painted ceilings enhanced by strategic pools of light and offset by movable panels artfully installed by minimalist master Tadao Ando. Hosting François Pinault's world-class contemporary-art collection, plus inspired travelling shows, Palazzo Grassi is the one place where Venice's past and future make perfect sense together – at least until Pinault unveils the Ando-redesigned Punta della Dogana (p114) in 2009. See p26 for more on the Grassi.

SANTA MARIA DEL GIGLIO

Campo di Santa Maria Zobenigo 2543; admission €3, with Chorus pass free; ☼ 10am-5pm Mon-Sat; ☷ Santa Maria del Giglio

A small baroque neighbourhood church from the outside, Santa Maria del Giglio is a small wonder inside, with a 10th-century Byzantine layout and intriguing works by three European masters.

Hiding behind the altar is Veronese's *Madonna with Child,* with Tintoretto's *Four Evangelists* flanking the organ. The Molin Chapel is a pretty piece of nepotism, with a ceiling painted by Jacopo Tintoretto's son Domenico; it's upstaged, however, by a small painting of Mary with Jesus and St John by the master of roly-poly gorgeousness, Peter Paul Rubens.

◉ SANTO STEFANO
Campo Santo Stefano 3825; church free, museum €3, with Chorus pass free; ☾ **10am-5pm Mon-Sat;** 🚶 **Accademia**
The timber ceilings of Venice's larger churches were made by boat builders, and here the *carena di nave* (ship's-keel) ceiling gives the impression that you're standing under an especially fine boat turned upside down for repairs. Duck into the side room to see two moving, brooding Tintoretto canvases: *The Last Supper,* with a ghostly little dog begging for bread, and the mostly black *Washing of the Feet.* The cloisters feature Antonio Canova's precocious 1808 funerary stelae for Giorgio Falier, showing women wrapped in cloaks and their own grief, alongside Tullio Lombardo's 1505 saint, which has such limpid, lovely upturned eyes that Titian referenced the piece for his Madonna in I Frari (p84).

🛍 SHOP
🛍 ARCOBALENO *Art Supplies*
☎ **041 5236818; Calle delle Botteghe 3457;** ☾ **9.30am-1.30pm & 3-7pm Mon-Sat;** 🚶 **Accademia**

After umpteen Venetian art masterpieces, anyone's fingers will start twitching for a paintbrush. With its shelves stocked with jars of all the essential pigments – Titian red, Tiepolo sky blue, Veronese rose and Tintoretto teal – Arcobaleno provides all the raw materials needed to start your own Venetian art movement.

🛍 EPICENTRO *Gifts, Homewares*
☎ **041 5226864; Calle dei Fabbri 932;** ☾ **3-7pm Mon, 9.30am-1.30pm & 3-7pm Tue-Sat;** 🚶 **Vallaresso**
How could you possibly survive without that Alessi-designed soy-sauce decanter shaped like a hummingbird? Epicentro provides every designer household item you never knew you needed, plus the entire Alessi back catalogue of monkey-shaped sugar bowls and toothbrush-hugging trolls, all crammed into one delightful little storefront.

🛍 FIORELLA GALLERY *Fashion*
☎ **041 5209228; www.fiorellagallery .com; Campo Santo Stefano 2806;** ☾ **3-7pm Mon, 9.30am-1.30pm & 3.30-7pm Tue-Sat;** 🚶 **Accademia**
At Fiorella, high-heeled doge mannequins show off subversive Venetian fashions hell-bent on bringing out your inner rock star. Smoking jackets are made of crushed silk velvets in louche

Crazy eyes: eyeball mannequins at Fiorella Gallery

jewellery to the next level – but prices starting at €35 are surprisingly down to earth, especially this close to San Marco.

LE BOTTEGHE
Gifts, Sustainable Shopping
☎ 041 5227545; Ponte di Rialto 5164;
🕐 10am-7pm Mon-Sat; 🚢 Rialto

Italian design meets global awareness at this fair-trade boutique on the steps of the Rialto. Sleek foldable straw hats made by a Bangladeshi collective in rich shades of saffron and fuchsia are just right for gondola rides, while African beaded clutches practically demand a date at La Fenice.

LEGATORIA PIAZZESI
Paper Crafts
☎ 041 5221202; www.legatoriapiazzesi.it; Campiello Feltrina 2511c; 🕐 varies; 🚢 Santa Maria del Giglio

This is the most eccentric shop in Venice – and that's saying something. A specialist in hand-stamped and marbled paper since 1851, this historic stationer sells photo albums, travel journals and book stands made from paper, and offers some esoteric add-on services, such as handwriting analysis and character readings. It opens when it likes, making every purchase seem somehow fated. Ask about paper-making classes and phrenology sessions.

shades of lavender and blood red, and are then printed by hand with baroque wallpaper patterns and a Fiorella signature: wide-eyed rats. Prices start in the hundreds of euros, but check out your reflection in the graffitied Ettore Sottsass mirror and tell us you're not impressed.

GLORIA ASTOLFO *Jewellery*
☎ 041 5206827; Calle Frezzeria 1581;
🕐 9.30am-1.30pm & 3-7pm Mon-Sat;
🚢 Vallaresso

Chandelier earrings straight out of a Venetian painting and collars of cascading pearls that would blend in with the baroque decor at La Fenice take handcrafted beadwork

📖 LIBRERIA STUDIUM *Books*
☎ 041 5222382; Calle Canonica 337; 🕑 9am-7.30pm Mon-Sat, 9.30am-1.30pm Sun; 🚉 San Zaccaria

This place has floor-to-ceiling holiday reads, including a large selection of literature in English that extends well beyond pulpy best-sellers, a section on Italian cuisine ranging from mouth-watering coffee-table books to scholarly tracts, plus a respectably vast Lonely Planet selection (not that we're biased). The book-loving staff can pluck obscure titles from high shelves for you with instant recall.

🔲 MA.RE *Glass*
☎ 041 5231191; www.mareglass.com; Via Larga XXII Marzo 2088; 🕑 10am-7pm Mon-Sat; 🚉 Santa Maria del Giglio

To appreciate the range of contemporary glass-designer talent on Murano without actually going there, check out this splashy showroom. Blown, etched, clear and boldly coloured: there's nothing these local designers won't do to turn glass into high-modernist objects. The limited-edition etched wineglasses by Salviati (€45 each) are the kind of glasses that are trotted out only for honoured guests who never gesture wildly while drinking.

🔲 MALIPARMI *Fashion*
☎ 041 5285608; www.maliparmi.it; Calle Teatro Goldoni 4600a; 🕑 10am-7pm Mon-Sat; 🚉 Santa Maria del Giglio

This is smart, breezy chic that's just right for urban islanders from Manhattan to Venice. Specialising in luxe looks with surprisingly uncouture price tags, this Padua-based designer has cuts that drape just so, fabrics that feel good to the touch, and an upscale-playful colour sensibility that brings to mind Missoni and Miu Miu.

🔲 MICROMEGA OTTICA *Eyeglasses*
☎ 041 2960765; www.micromegaottica.com; Campo di Santa Maria del Giglio 2436; 🕑 10.30am-7pm Mon-Sat, 11am-7pm Sun; 🚉 Santa Maria del Giglio

Frames by this eyewear designer are made of natural materials – horn, gold wire, a twig stripped of its bark – and constructed without hinges or stress points for durability and comfort. Lenses are laser cut into simple shapes or free-form designs, including leaf-shaped lenses. This is sculpture for your face, and it's priced accordingly: glasses are €600 and up.

🔲 MILLEVINI *Wine*
☎ 041 5206090; Ramo del Fontego dei Turchi 5362; 🕑 9am-1.30pm & 3.30-7pm Mon-Sat; 🚉 Rialto

This wine-cave-cum-industrial-warehouse has small-producer labels and Venetian vintages, adding a touch of class amid the Rialto T-shirt kiosks and kitschy cafes. Well-versed staff help you choose from bottles lit like offerings to the gods, and will give you the inside scoop on upcoming wine tastings.

📖 MONDADORI *Books, Music*
☎ 041 5222193; Salizada San Moisè 1345; ⏱ 10am-10pm Mon-Sat, 3-8pm Sun; ⚓ Vallaresso

Come for the books and music, stay for the architecture, boozing and schmoozing. The selection of CDs, mags, DVDs and novels in this Italian chain is plenty engrossing, but even precision-target shoppers will linger in the glassed-in converted cinema, which also houses Bacaro (p54), and hosts literary events and photography shows.

👓 OTTICA CARRARO *Eyeglasses*
☎ 041 5204258; www.otticacarraro.it; Calle della Mandola 3706; ⏱ 9am-1pm & 3.30-7pm Mon-Sat; ⚓ Sant'Angelo

Lost your sunglasses on the Lido? Never fear: Ottico Carraro can make you a custom pair within 24 hours. Styles range from flashy 1980s-style shades to arty matte-rubber frames that look like they were crafted from gumdrops.

👕 VENETIA STUDIUM
Fashion, Homewares
☎ 041 5236953; www.venetiastudium .com; Palazzo Zuccato, Via Larga XXII

Marzo 2425; ⏱ 10am-7pm Mon-Sat; ⚓ Santa Maria del Giglio

Get that 'just got in from Monaco for my art opening' look beloved of bohemians who marry well. The high-drama Delphos tunic dresses make anyone look like a high-maintenance modern dancer or art collector (Isadora Duncan and Peggy Guggenheim were both fans), while the hand-stamped silk-velvet bags (prices start at €50) are more arty than ostentatious.

🍴 EAT

🍰 ANDREA ZANIN *Pastries* €
☎ 041 5224803; Campo San Luca 4589; ⏱ 9am-7pm Mon-Sat; ⚓ Rialto

Two-bite treats served on a sparkly bar with a powerful espresso are Venice's answer to Prozac. Everything here is stylish and delightful: nibbles of sponge cake with lemon mousse, tiny chocolate cups filled with three kinds of mousse and topped with gold leaf, and sesame *gianduia* (chocolate-nut fondant) truffles that are ideal for intermission at La Fenice.

🥪 CAFFE MANDOLA
Sandwiches €
☎ 041 5237624; Calle della Mandola 3630; ⏱ 9am-7pm Mon-Sat; ⚓ Vallaresso

Sandwiches on fresh focaccia are the speciality here: inspired fillings include tangy tuna and capers,

Giovanni d'Este

Sommelier and happy-hour mind-reader at Osteria I Rusteghi (p54)

Bring your compass True Venetian *osterie* [restaurant-bars] are always hidden, so you have to work a bit to get to the good stuff. **Guessing your order** Americans enjoy layered reds, like amarone; the French are used to softer wines such as ripasso, made with young valpolicella and skins from amarone. But everyone likes soave and prosecco. **Surprising Veneto wines** Pramaggiore cabernet franc is like a beautiful woman: it's very rounded and immediately gets your attention. Refosco is an ancient wine; it's in our DNA here. Our merlot is extremely elegant, with body, acidity and strength of character – it makes other merlots seem young and naive. **Anything but...** Dry spumante with cake, how horrendous! The sweetness cancels out the subtle spumante. Fragolino [strawberry-flavoured wine] is fine, but Venetians don't dunk biscuits in it. *Sgroppino* [lemon sorbet with prosecco and vodka] is ideal for cleaning your palate between courses.

and lean bresaola (air-dried beef), rocket and seasoned grana padano cheese. Stools provide sweet relief for tired feet if you grab your *panini* (sandwiches) outside the lunch peak and happy hour.

CAVA TAPPI

Classic Venetian, Sandwiches €
☎ 041 2960252; Campo della Guerra 525-526; 11.15am-4pm Tue-Thu, 11.15-4pm & 7-10pm Fri & Sat; San Zaccaria

A stone's throw from Piazza San Marco but a world apart from over-done decor and dire tourist menus, Cava Tappi is a sleek charmer with seasonal dishes, a terrific selection of wines by the glass, and that rarest of San Marco finds: tasty meals that regularly come in under €10. You don't even need to look at the menu: just order the pasta or risotto of the day, ask your server to manage the wine pairing, and get the sheep's cheese drizzled with honey for dessert.

ENOTECA AL VOLTO

Cicheti, Classic Venetian €€
☎ 041 5228945; Calle Cavalli 4081; 11am-2pm & 5-9pm Tue-Sat; Rialto

Join the crowd working their way through the vast selection of wine and *cicheti* (Venetian tapas) at the bar, or show up early to nab a table in the snug wood-beamed back room, where you'll feel like

Feel that warm glow inside at Enoteca Al Volto

a stowaway in a ship's hold and eat like a captain. The portions of pasta with clams and white wine would satisfy even hard-working gondolieri, while thick steaks are served in a puddle of juice with a proper glass of amarone.

OSTERIA ALLA BOTTE

Cicheti, Classic Venetian €€
☎ 041 5209775; Calle della Bissa 5482; 11am-3pm & 5.30-10pm Mon-Wed, Fri & Sat, 11am-3pm Sun; Rialto

Budget gourmets throng the bar, pairing each round of *cicheti* with a different wine by the glass – there are more than 25 on offer here. The dining room is less busy and tends to stick to basic crowd-pleasing

SESTIERI

SAN MARCO

pastas with seafood, though you might find an authentic plate of tripe if you're lucky.

🍴 OSTERIA I RUSTEGHI
Cicheti €€
☎ 041 5232205; Corte del Tentor 5513; ⏱ 10.30am-3pm & 6-9pm Mon-Fri; 🚇 Rialto

An *osteria* owned by fourth-generation wine specialists who have their own butcher in Tuscany? That explains the outstanding wine and *cicheti* selection. Baguette slices are creatively topped with seafood, grilled vegetables and truffles, but the meat options are the breakaway hits here: boar salami, pancetta and a velvety *lardo di Colonnata* (cured pork fat) that will win you over to lard. Ask Giovanni to choose your wine, and he'll give you a long look to sum up your character before presenting you with his selection – high compliments being a big-hearted, mature raboso del Piave or a clever refosco.

🍴 VINI DA ARTURO *Steak* €€€
☎ 041 5286974; Calle degli Assassini 3656; ⏱ 7-11pm Mon-Sat; 🚇 Sant'Angelo

You could flirt with the pasta menu, but everyone in this corridor-sized eight-table restaurant comes for the same reason: the steak. Studded with green peppercorns, soused in brandy and mustard, or rare on the bone, these thick, tender slabs could be cut with a butter knife. *And* they deserve Hollywood credits – your host will happily trot out irrefutable proof that Nicole Kidman actually eats and that director Joel Silver managed to escape *The Matrix* for dinner here.

🍸 DRINK

🍸 B BAR *Lounge*
☎ 041 2406842; www.bauervenezia.com; Campo San Moisè 1459; ⏱ 6pm-1am Tue-Sun; 🚇 San Marco, Vallaresso

Pose as glitterati at your booth in the gold-mosaic B Bar, where top-shelf cocktails are thoughtfully served with bar nibbles and the piano player plays softly so as not to upstage VIP guests such as yourself. There's an entire menu of creative twists on the classic Venetian *spritz* (prosecco-based cocktail), including the bittersweet Rialto, with prosecco, gin and a splash of grenadine.

🍸 BACARO *Lounge*
☎ 041 2960687; Salizada San Moisè 1345; ⏱ 9am-2am; 🚇 San Marco, Vallaresso

Bacaro has good looks and smarts too: the bar is a shimmering mosaic oval that reflects well on you, and the company you'll keep is terribly clever, especially once the crowd moves here after literary events at Mondadori (p51), next door.

SAN MARCO

☿ BAR ALL'ANGOLO *Cafe-Bar*

☎ 041 5220710; Campo Santo Stefano 3463; ☼ 8am-9pm Sun-Fri; ⚓ Accademia

Picture your neighbourhood joint, only with a glass case stuffed with tempting *tramezzini* (sandwiches), chic orange-velvet booths, and an ideal position for people-watching on a buzzing, lively piazza. Stick around for a *spritz* at 6.30pm, when the local crowd arrives en masse.

☿ HARRY'S BAR *Lounge*

☎ 041 5285777; Calle Vallaresso 1323; ☼ noon-11pm; ⚓ San Marco, Vallaresso

Since almost every major 20th-century American talent has imbibed here – Charlie Chaplin, Ernest Hemingway, Truman Capote, Orson Welles – there's a theory that genius is stirred into these cocktails. Sounds like a good excuse for a drink. Yes, the €18 peach-and-prosecco Bellinis invented here are that good, and yes, meals here are among the most expensive in Venice and hence Europe (though in light of the American mortgage crisis, Harry's is offering 20% off the bill to US patrons). But the surprise is how down to earth the whole operation is, with simple bistro chairs, small tables set close together, and straightforward service with zero affectation. Harry's Bar is now an empire, with lo-cations in London and Hong Kong, and packaged pasta sold under the Cipriani label, but there's no substitute for the original.

☿ TORINO@NOTTE *Cafe-Bar*

☎ 041 5223914; Campo San Luca 4592; ☼ 8pm-1am Tue-Sat; ⚓ Rialto

Freeform, eclectic and loud, Torino adds an element of the unexpected to postdinner drinks in otherwise staid San Marco. On any given night you can enjoy a €2 to €4 drink with music provided by a live band, a spontaneous college-student singalong or a collection of scratchy reggae records played by a friend of the bartender.

☿ VINO VINO *Wine Bar*

☎ 041 2417688; Calle della Veste 2007a; ☼ 12.30-3pm & 7.30-11pm Wed-Mon; ⚓ Santa Maria del Giglio

Navigate the vast selection of wines by the glass with your server's help, or just ask your neighbours what they're having – it's that kind of place. There's an increasingly expansive menu of Venetian classics such as octopus salad and *sarde in saor* (sardines in an onion marinade) and fancier fare involving guinea fowl and suckling pig, but it's the selection of 300 wines that have made this place an institution for visitors and Venetians alike.

SESTIERI

SAN MARCO

PLAY

AURORA CAFFÈ
Cultural Events, Live Music

☎ 041 5286405; www.aurora.st; Piazza San Marco 48-50; ⏱ noon-2am Wed-Sun; 🚊 San Marco, Vallaresso

By day it blends in with the other cafes on the piazza, doling out pricey cappuccinos to the tourist trade – but after 8pm this plucky little venue is almost single-handedly responsible for signs of life on Piazza San Marco. Sunday nights pull in crowds with local musicians, exhibitions of emerging artists and €2 drinks between 9pm and 10pm. On Thursday nights, photography and video-art events draw Venetians out of their garrets to flirt and discuss the meaning of life.

CAFFÈ FLORIAN
Classical Music, Jazz

☎ 041 5205641; Piazza San Marco 56-59; ⏱ 10am-11pm Tue-Thu; 🚊 San Marco, Vallaresso

Tango, anyone? Without the daily accompaniment of the Caffè Florian house orchestra, the sun might not be allowed to set in Venice. Florian mostly sticks to rituals established in 1720 – unctuously charming uniformed waiters, gooey hot chocolate served on a silver tray, lovers canoodling on plush banquettes indoors – but has updated its musical repertoire to about 1950

to include jazz and Latin numbers. Since that hot chocolate will cost you €10 (with a €6 surcharge for piazza seating), you may as well stick around for the sunset grand finale, when the fading light illuminates the Basilica di San Marco's portal mosaics. It's an unforgettable experience – except for the bathrooms, which are cramped and grey. You'll be expected to leave a tip for the surly *signora* handing out towels.

CENTRALE *DJs, Live Music*

☎ 041 2960664; www.centrale-lounge.com; Piscina Frezzeria 1659b; ⏱ 6.30pm-2am Mon-Sat; 🚊 San Marco, Vallaresso

The optional bodyguard service may seem a bit much but, with its nocturnal instincts and low-key cool, Centrale is Venice's VIP magnet. Within these exposed-brick walls you might spot Juliette Binoche, Spike Lee and sundry Italian moguls, all moodily lit by Murano chandeliers. Meal prices are high, but Centrale draws late-night crowds for drinks, snacks, chill-out DJ sets and occasional live music.

MUSICA A PALAZZO *Opera*

☎ 340 9717272; www.musicapalazzo.com; Palazzo Barbarigo-Minotto, Fondamenta Duodo o Barbarigo 2504; ticket €45; ⏱ doors open 8pm; 🚊 Santa Maria del Giglio

In these intimate settings, the soprano's high notes might make

Strut your stuff outside Caffè Florian

you fear for your wineglass, and the thundering baritone is felt in the base of your spine. The 1½-hour show feels more like a decadent baroque party than a performance, with 70 guests – wineglasses in tow – following opera singers and orchestra from receiving room to salon to private quarters. The singers are in modern dress, but instead of appearing theatrical or anachronistic, they seem to be pouring their hearts out, pleading their cases with Verdi and drawing you into their Rossini intrigues.

TEATRO LA FENICE
Classical Music, Opera
☎ 041 786611; www.teatrolafenice.it; Campo San Fantin 1965; ticket price varies; ⏰ varies; ⚓ Santa Maria del Giglio
International opera reputations are still made and lost on this postage stamp of a stage, just as they have been for centuries, despite two fires and countless backstage intrigues. La Fenice (the Phoenix) has risen from the ashes of a 1996 arson, and the grand new theatre remains true to the baroque blueprints of 1836. The stage is encircled by box seating dripping with gold and decorated with sweet-faced babies rather precociously weaving garlands and playing musical instruments.
Tours (☎ 041 2424; adult/student €7/5) are possible with advance booking by phone, but the best way to see La Fenice is with the *loggione*, opera buffs that pass judgment on productions from on high in the top-tier cheap seats. In between performances and in the opera off season, symphonies and chamber-music concerts are irresistible draws at La Fenice.

>CASTELLO

Sailors, saints and modern artists have made Castello what it is today: a waterfront home to earthy *osterie* (restaurant-bars), ethereal icons and the show-stopper that is the Biennale. Churches are gilt to the hilt, historic four-star hotels sprawl along the Grand Canal waterfront, and the Biennale pavilions are showpieces of modern architecture. Venice's Armenian and Greek communities once lived in these winding lanes alongside Turkish and Syrian merchants, bringing to the neighbourhood a cosmopolitan flair that's still noticeable in local restaurants, as well as even more glittering icons. But Castello has proven that it's possible to be refined in the extreme without losing that vital roughness around the edges: some 5000 shipbuilders once worked here in the Arsenale, building the fleet that extended Venice's empire to Constantinople. Traces of those glory days can be found in the Museo Storico Navale and in the odd bawdy joke at happy hour.

CASTELLO

◎ SEE
Biennale Pavilions...........1 G6
Fondazione Querini
Stampalia...................2 B2
Museo della Fondazione
Querini-Stampalia.....(see 2)
Museo delle Icone 3 C3
Museo Storico Navale.....4 D4
Ospedaletto...................5 B2
San Zaccaria 6 B3
Sotoportego dei Preti 7 C3
Zanipolo 8 B1

🛍 SHOP
Arte Vetro Murano 9 B3
Banco 10.....................10 C3
Giovanna Zanella 11 A2
Metropoli Scarpe.........12 B2
Parole e Musica 13 A2
Schegge.....................14 B2
Sigfrido Cipolato 15 A3

🍴 EAT
Aciugheta 16 B3
Al Covo.......................17 C3
Conca d'Oro 18 B3
Enoteca Mascareta.......19 B2
Il Ridotto 20 B3

Osteria di Santa
Marina 21 A2
Taverna San Lio 22 A2

🍸 DRINK
Florian Arte Caffè.........(see 2)
Obillok 23 B1
Paradiso 24 F6
Taverna l'Olandese
Volante 25 A2

⭐ PLAY
Jazz in Venice 26 B3

Please see over for map

⊙ SEE

⊙

www.labiennale.org; 🏛 Giardini
In between the Art Biennale (in
odd-numbered years) and the
architecture showcase (in even
years), the public gardens here
are for lovers. Gothically romantic
vines creep up to cover the Pal-
ladian-style British Pavilion, and
picnickers canoodle between the
mosaic-detailed secessionist-style
Austro-Hungarian Pavilion and
the disappointingly derivative US
Pavilion. Pavilions cover just about
every major modernist movement
and construction material, from the
'70s ski-lodge stylings of the timber
Canadian building to the metal-clad
Korean Pavilion in a converted elec-
trical plant. James Stirling's 1991
Book Pavilion is more interesting
from the inside, Italy's blindingly
white Fascist-era pavilion is grandi-
ose and Peter Cox's 1988 Australian
Pavilion (intended to be temporary)
looks like a mobile home – but it's
hard to compete with the home-
town favourite Carlo Scarpa's clever
raw-concrete-and-glass Venezuelan
Pavilion from 1954, which still looks
avant-garde. See p17 and p29 for
more on the Biennale.

⊙

☎ 041 2711411; www.querinistamp
alia.it; Ponte Querini 5252; adult/student

€8/6; ☼ 10am-8pm Tue-Thu, 10am-
10pm Fri & Sat, 10am-7pm Sun; ⚓ San
Zaccaria
Modern meets baroque in this
16th-century *palazzo* (palace or
mansion), which was updated by
Carlo Scarpa in the 1940s, and
had a Mario Botta–designed cafe
(p68) and bookshop added in the
1990s. The middle floors preserve
the graces of bygone centuries,
with porcelain displays on silk-clad
walls and an entire Giovanni Bellini room; downstairs, Scarpa's Is-
lamic-inspired water channels run
through the ground floor and into
the courtyard fountain. Top-floor
modern-art shows are hit-and-
miss, but coffee in Scarpa's garden
is a must. Stick around on Friday
and Saturday for concerts held in
the baroque music room.

⊙

☎ 041 5226581; www.istitutoellen
ico.org; Campiello dei Greci 3412;
adult/student €4/2; ☼ 9am-12.30pm
& 1.30-4.30pm Mon-Sat, 9am-5pm Sun;
⚓ San Zaccaria
Glowing colours and all-seeing
eyes fill the gallery of the Museum of Icons, a treasure trove of
elegant Greek icons made in 14th-
to 17th-century Italy. Especially
impressive is the expressive *San
Giovanni Climaco*, which shows
the saintly author of a Greek
spiritual guide distracted from his

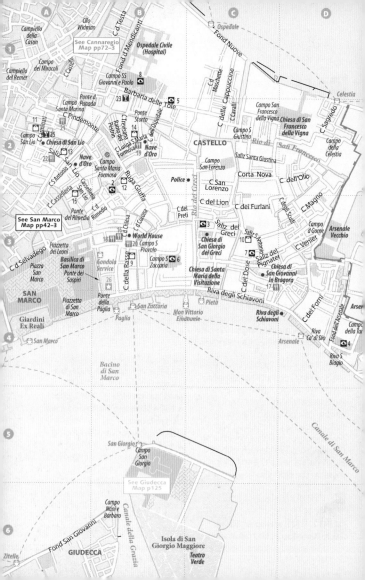

ork by visions of souls diving into hell. The building itself is a monument to the city's religious tolerance: this seat of Venice's Greek Orthodox community was built by Baldassare Longhena, Venice's official architect, and served as a hospital for the poor into the 20th century.

◉ MUSEO STORICO NAVALE

☎ 041 5200276; Fondamenta dell'Arsenale 2148; admission €3; 🕑 8.45am-1.30pm Mon-Fri, 8.45am-1pm Sat; 🚇 Arsenale

The improbable tale of Venice's seafaring empire and the city's lingering fascination with boats unfolds in rambling fashion across four floors and 42 rooms of painstakingly detailed boat models and fearsome weaponry – which was rarely used within Venice, but was kept on hand at the Arsenale, just in case. The fanciest boat is the model of the *bucintoro* (ducal barge), used in ceremonial occasions such as the Sposalizio del Mar (Wedding to the Sea; p28). But Peggy Guggenheim's gondola isn't shabby either, and the

Pimp my *bucintoro* (ducal barge)? Check out the the dogi's gilt-y pleasures at the Museo Storico Navale

THE ORPHAN ORCHESTRAS OF VENICE

ocean liners and WWII battleships are fascinating.

☎ 041 5322920; Barbaria delle Tole 6691; admission €3; 🕑 3.30-6.30pm Fri & Sat Apr-Oct, 3-6pm Fri & Sat Nov-Mar; 🚤 Ospedale
So much for Rome's attempt to limit Venice's love affair with music: a musical theme runs right through the 1664 Longhena-designed chapel and music room in this home for orphans and the infirm. The chapel is uplifting by design, with a trumpeting angel flitting overhead, and the mighty organ reflected on the ceiling to draw the eye upward. Jacopo

Guarana painted the frescoes that cover the Sala da Musica, where female orphans performed in celebrated concerts (see above).

☎ 041 5221257; Campo San Zaccaria 4693; Cappella di Sant'Atanasio €1; 🕑 10am-noon & 4-6pm Mon-Sat, 4-6pm Sun; 🚤 San Zaccaria
If these walls could talk, they'd tell tales of a former life as a convent for the daughters of Venice's up-per crust, who passed their time here in prayer, concerts and rather scandalous masked balls. The influence of this church is visible in its wealth of art: a 12th-century Roman-Byzantine mosaic floor,

View the wealth of art at San Zaccaria (p63)

the dazzling gilt polyptych in the Golden Chapel, Bellini's melancholy enthroned Madonna, and Giambattista Tiepolo's version of the flight into Egypt in a Venetian boat. Don't miss Antonio Vivarini's 1443 painting of St Sabina, who keeps her cool as angels buzz around her head like lagoon mosquitoes.

SOTOPORTEGO DEI PRETI

off Salizada dell Pignater; 🚇 Arsenale
Down the steps and under the arch of this *sotoportego* (passageway), there's a heart-shaped reddish stone the size of a hand. Legend has it that couples who touch it together remain in love forever – but, if you're not ready to commit just yet, it's a nice private spot for a smooch.

ZANIPOLO

Basilica dei Santi Giovanni e Paolo; ☎ 041 5235913; Campo Santi Giovanni e Paolo 6363; admission €2.50; ⏱ 9.30am-6pm Mon-Sat, 1-6pm Sun; 🚇 Ospedale
This generous Gothic church is big enough to house several masterpieces, 25 tombs of dogi (Venice's leaders) by such notable artists as Nicolo Pisano and Tullio Lombardo, and examples of most major architectural styles to hit Venice since work began on the church in 1333. The first chapel on the right holds Giambattista Lorenzetti's baroque relief of *Jesus the Navigator*, with Jesus looking at the moon and searching the stars like a Venetian sea captain. Another wonderful work is Guido Reni's *San Giuseppe*, showing Joseph exchanging tender, adoring looks with baby Jesus. Since the church is connected to Venice's main hospital, the Ospedale Civile, one of the most popular shrines is the one to Venetian James Salomoni, patron of cancer patients, whose own wounds are said to have emitted a 'heavenly fragrance' after his death. But the most spectacular piece is Paolo Veronese's ceiling depicting the rosy Virgin being crowned by cherubs as she

ascends a staircase, with angels flipping with the joy of it all.

🛍 SHOP

⬛ ARTE VETRO

☎ 041 5237514; www.artevetromurano .com; Calle della Rasse 4613; ⏲ 10am-1pm & 3-6pm Mon-Sat; 🚉 San Zaccaria
Shatter glass conventions with new styles by emerging Murano glass designers: Davide Penso makes a necklace of flat puddles of orange glass that have a molten-lava look about them, while Artematte's deliberately mismatched lampwork glass earrings will earn you double takes at Biennale art openings.

⬛ BANCO 10
Fashion, Sustaine

☎ 041 5221439; Salizada Sant'Antonio 3478a; ⏲ 3.30-6pm Mon, 10am-1pm & 3.30-6pm Tue-Sat; 🚉 San Zaccaria
Prison orange is so over. All the swirly skirts, sleek jackets, tapestry handbags and diva dresses in this nonprofit boutique are made as part of a retraining program at the women's prison on Giudecca, funding their continuing career training and reintegration into society after release. Sumptuous silks, velvets and tapestry are donated by Fortuny and Bevilacqua, designs are created by female inmates, and volunteers sell them in this truly inspired boutique. Even La Fenice

has dressed its divas in cc made through the program.

⬛

☎ 041 5235500; Calle Carminati 5641; ⏲ 9.30am-1pm & 3-7pm; 🚉 Rialto
Woven, sculpted, and crested like birds, Zanella's shoes practically demand that red carpets unfurl before you. The Venetian designer custom-makes the shoes, so the answer is always, 'Yes, you can get those peep-toe numbers in yellow and grey, size 12, extra narrow.' It'll cost you of course, but at least you won't be upstaged by Angelina Jolie in the same pair at the Venice Film Festival.

⬛

☎ 041 5235588; Calle Scaletta 4946; ⏲ 10am-6.30pm Mon-Sat; 🚉 Rialto
You knew there had to be a designer shoe outlet in Venice. Colours are loud and styles aren't shy – think yellow patent-leather flats with pilgrim buckles, or powder-pink wrestling boots – but, with prices from €39 to €59, budget-minded fashionistas can afford to take style risks.

⬛

☎ 041 5235010; www.intermusic.biz; Salizada San Lio 5673; ⏲ 10am-7.30pm Mon-Sat, 11am-7.30pm Sun; 🚉 Rialto
Head to this store to take Venice's music home with you. Specialising

CASTELLO

...pera,
...s and
...are

...a Santa
Maria Formosa... ...9am-9pm
Mon-Sat; 🚹 Rialto

Go incognito in style with this shop's highly original masquerade masks, which are inspired by influences as diverse as Gothic architecture and the paintings of Amedeo Modigliani. Well into the night, you'll find this dedicated mother-daughter team wielding tiny paintbrushes, coaxing minute baroque tendrils into bloom along the side of a mask.

A dazzling display of Carnevale masks

📿 SIGFRIDO CIPOLATO
Jewellery

☎ 041 5228437; San Lio Caselleria 5336; 🕑 10am-1pm & 3-7pm Mon-Sat; 🚹 San Zaccaria

The window display here looks like a baroque jewel box: chandelier earrings ending in tiny gold skulls, Fabergé-incised enamel rings with emeralds, free-form pearls set in diamonds. Though they may look like heirlooms, these small wonders were created by jeweller Sigfridio, who uses techniques handed down through generations.

🍴 EAT

🍴 ACIUGHETA *Cicheti* €€

☎ 041 5224292; Campo Santi Filippo e Giacomo 4357; 🕑 noon-3pm & 6pm-midnight Mon-Sat; 🚹 San Zaccaria

Ignore the pizza menu: why choose just one dish when you could go for a range of minipizzas, meatballs, crostini and other *cicheti* (Venetian tapas) with a good glass of wine? You can stand at the marble bar or, if you come early or late enough, you might be able to grab a seat in the sleekly remodelled back room amid the throngs of regulars.

🍴 AL COVO
Invèntive Venetian €€€

☎ 041 5223812; www.ristorantealcovo .com; Campiello della Pescaria 3968; 🕑 7-11pm Fri-Tue; 🚹 Arsenale

This place has all the makings of a classic Venetian *osteria* – low-beamed ceilings, exposed brick wall, regulars in the corner – but its typical dishes come with a twist. Caprese salad gets the Covo treatment, with basil and *mozzarella di bufala* (buffalo mozzarella) served with a heavenly cherry-tomato jelly; squid-ink pasta comes with clams and zucchini flowers; and Adriatic tuna is accompanied by five sauces. The high prices are understandable given the robust flavours of the top-quality ingredients from around the lagoon (which are especially notable in the mixed seafood antipasti), and are offset by the incredible range of reasonably priced limited-production wine – the staff will open any wine for you and only charge you for half the full bottle.

🍴 CONCA D'ORO *Pizza* €€
☎ 041 5229293; Campo Santi Filippo e Giacomo 4338; 🕑 noon-3.30pm & 6.30-10.30pm; 🚊 San Zaccaria
Pizza is not a local speciality – in case you hadn't guessed from the cardboard pies you'll find at eateries pandering to the tourist trade around San Marco – but this place is the exception. This local joint right behind San Marco brought pizza to Venice in 1960, and has been slinging generous thin-crust pies with creative toppings ever since. It's not

especially quick about it, though, so relax and enjoy the sun in the piazza and the Italian ska blaring on the stereo.

🍴 ENOTECA MASCARETA *Cicheti* €€
☎ 041 5230744; Calle Lunga Santa Maria Formosa 5183; 🕑 7pm-2am Fri-Tue; 🚊 San Zaccaria
Mauro, the host here, is quintessentially Venetian, with humorously blunt opinions about wine and food pairings. *Primi* (first courses) and mains are pricey, but the early-evening *cicheti* and appetiser platters of meats and cheeses could pass for a meal, and Mauro can hardly be stopped from pouring you his choice from 100 wines for €2 to €3.50 a glass. In good weather, the outdoor bar is the place to feast on *cicheti* and an *ombra* (glass) or two of organic wine for under €10.

🍴 IL RIDOTTO *Inventive Venetian* €€€
☎ 041 5208280; www.ilridotto.com; Campo Santi Filippo e Giacomo 4509; 🕑 7-11pm Thu, noon-3pm & 7-11pm Fri-Tue; 🚊 San Zaccaria
From an open kitchen the size of a closet comes a parade of tasty small plates: a dollop of savoury Tuscan bread pudding, Venetian seafood composed into a glistening mosaic, a silky *panna cotta*. Mains

Wine and pizza: the perfect Italian lunch

fixed-price menu or the all-out adventure of the €75 tasting menu, where each course brings an artful dab of reinvented local fare – a prawn in a nest of shaved red pepper, black squid-ink ravioli stuffed with *branzino* (sea bass), artichoke and soft-shell crab with zucchini *saor* (onion marinade). Dessert is a must, especially the homemade gelati and the hot chocolate pie.

TAVERNA SAN LIO
Inventive Venetian   €€
☎ 041 2770669; www.tavernasanlio.com; Salizada San Lio 5547; ☺ 7-11pm Tue-Sat; ⚑ Rialto
Modern without losing Venice's essential quirkiness, this place handles its seafood dishes delicately: go with the seasonal choice of scallops with thyme, pink pepper and saffron, or with homemade sea bream ravioli with a mint-pesto sauce, paired with the sprightly house pinot grigio. Low wood tables encourage diners to lean toward one another conspiratorially, amoeba-shaped lamps set the mood for free-form conversation and huge windows let you in on the catwalk action outdoors.

are less satisfying and quite pricey, so you might want to stick to an assortment of antipasti and *primi*. There are only five tables set close together, which makes the frosty service puzzling – but the ever present chef is warm and attentive, and the decor of gossamer veils and exposed brick sets the scene for modern Venetian romance.

OSTERIA DI SANTA MARINA
Inventive Venetian   €€€
☎ 041 5285239; Campo Santa Marina 5911; ☺ 6-11pm Mon, noon-3pm & 6-11pm Tue-Sat; ⚑ Rialto
Don't be fooled by the casual piazza seating and simple dark-wood interiors: this restaurant is saving up all the drama for your plate. Given the à la carte prices, you might as well go for the €55

⚑ DRINK
FLORIAN ARTE CAFFÈ
Cafe-Bar
☎ 041 5289758; Fondazione Querini Stampalia, Ponte Querini 5252;

🕙 10am-7pm Tue-Thu, 10am-9pm Fri & Sat, 10am-6pm Sun; 🚹 San Zaccaria
Espresso with a side of architectural inspiration, please. Rainy days are right for hot chocolate inside Mario Botta's snug modernist cafe, with its white walls framed in black, polished-concrete floors and a harmonious, repeating-rectangle theme. Outside, Carlo Scarpa's clever Middle East–inspired concrete irrigation channels add industrial-Islamic cool to your *spritz* (prosecco-based cocktail) in the sunny garden.

🍸 OBILLOK *Cafe-Bar*
☎ 041 5284639; www.obillok.it; Campo Santi Giovanni e Paolo 6331; 🕙 11am-8pm; 🚹 Ospedale
Devastatingly handsome and artfully Venetian, this cafe-bar has oversized baroque flourishes stamped on the walls, Titian red chairs and a sculpted-brass bar where beer is served in leaning glasses. Looks aside, the macchiatos here are among Venice's best, and the mean *spritz* and sweet jazz pull in the crowds at happy hour.

🍸 PARADISO *Cafe-Bar*
☎ 335 6223079; Giardini Pubblici 1260; 🕙 9am-7pm; 🚹 Biennale
At Paradiso, curators woo shy artists on mod couches and star architects hold court under sun umbrellas, even between Biennales. The scene is fuelled by a steady stream of coffee and cocktails that cost less than you'd expect given the designer chairs, waterfront location and lack of competition – this is the only cafe within reach of anyone in stilettos at the Biennale.

🍸 TAVERNA L'OLANDESE VOLANTE *Pub*
☎ 041 5289349; Salizada San Lio 5658; 🕙 10am-2pm & 5pm-12.30am Mon-Sat, 10am-2pm Sun; 🚹 Rialto
Chaos reigns at the Flying Dutchman, where study-abroad students mingle easily and laugh loudly with local eccentrics over cheap beer. On summer nights, expect to go home happily hoarse.

🎭 PLAY
🎵 JAZZ IN VENICE *Jazz*
☎ 041 984252; www.collegiumducale .com; Prigioni Nuove; adult/student €25/20; 🕙 shows 6pm & 9pm; 🚹 San Zaccaria
Miles Davis' 'All Blues' takes on a whole new meaning when you're hearing the jazz standard in a jail cell. Offenders brought here in shackles a few centuries back might not have been in a position to appreciate the great acoustics, but concertgoers willingly make return visits to hear the bass boom off the vaulted ceilings and to take in moody piano solos that would be lost in a bar.

>CANNAREGIO

Anyone could adore Venice on looks alone, but in Cannaregio you'll fall for its personality. Located between extroverted San Marco and introverted Santa Croce, earthy Castello and saintly San Polo, Cannaregio combines all of its neighbours' personality quirks. Day trippers race along broad Strada Nova en route from the train to the Rialto, while just a few streets over, footsteps echo along moody stretches of Fondamenta della Misericordia without a T-shirt kiosk in sight. The Jewish Ghetto (p19) is a tribute to the tough, tolerant community of Cannaregio, who stuck it out on these malarial swamps; both top-floor synagogues and Gothic churches are an integral part of the scenery. At night, students from nearby Ca' Foscari University and visitors who are loath to leave converge on local *osterie* (restaurant-bars) for drinks, gossip and some of Venice's least-known and best-priced dinners.

CANNAREGIO

Please see over for map

◎ SEE

◎ CA' D'ORO

☎ 041 5222349; Calle di Ca' d'Oro 3932; www.cadoro.org, in Italian; adult/EU student under 26yr/EU under 18yr & over 65yr €5/2.50/free; ☼ 8.15am-2pm Mon, 8.15am-7.15pm Tue-Sun; ⚓ Ca' d'Oro

Napoleon had excellent taste in plunder, as this palace museum reveals. But until Baron Franchetti donated Ca' d'Oro to Venice as an art museum (along with his personal art collection), the paintings, reliefs and sculpture taken from Veneto churches during Napoleon's Italy conquest had to be warehoused at Milan's Brera museum. Collection highlights include Andrea Mantegna's magnificent altarpiece of a teeth-bearing, blood-dripping, arrow-riddled *St Sebastian*; Pietro Lombardo's tender *Madonna and Child* in glistening Carrara marble; and a faded but still sensuous nude on a fragment of a fresco by Giorgione. The palace itself is a masterwork of *palazzo* (palace or mansion) architecture, with its Gothic Grand Canal balcony and marble-mosaic ground floor, even though it was long ago stripped of the polychrome marble and gold-leaf cladding that gave it its name (House of Gold).

◎ CAMPO DEL GHETTO NUOVO

www.ghetto.it; ⚓ San Marcuola

Look around: this lopsided plaza that serves as a community playground was once the unofficial centre of Venice's shipping empire. Jews were originally only allowed to live in Giudecca, but Venice saw the benefit in keeping

Ponder dark history in a sunny spot on the Campo del Ghetto Nuovo

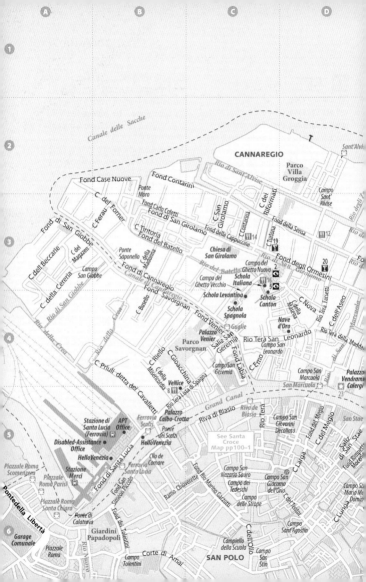

CANNAREGIO

Canale delle Sacche

Rio di Sant'Alvise

Sant'Alvise

Parco Villa Groggia

Campo Sant'Alvise

Fond Case Nuove

Fond Contarini

Ponte Moro

Fond Carlo Coletti

Fond di San Girolamo

C. San Girolamo

Fond delle Cappuccine

C. dei Riformati

Fond della Sensa

C. del Forner

C. Ferau

Fond di San Giobbe

C. Tintoria

Fond del Batello

Chiesa di San Girolamo

Tintoria

Rio degli

C. dei Magazen

C. dell'Beccarie

Ponte Saponello

Campo San Giobbe

Fond di Cannaregio

Rio del Batello

Campo del Ghetto Nuovo

Schola Italiana

Fond degli Ormesini

C. della Cereria

Fond Savorgnan

Campo del Ghetto Vecchio

Schola Levantina

Schola Canton

C. Nova

C. della Misericordia

Rio di San Giobbe

C. Bucelo

Fond Venier

Schola Spagnola

Nave d'Oro

Rio Terà San Leonardo

Rio Terà della Madda

Rio della Crea

Palazzo Venier

Guglie

Parco Savorgnan

Saliz San Geremia

Campo San Leonardo

C. Priuli detta dei Cavalletti

C. Riello

C. Gioacchina

Fond Labia

Campo San Geremia

Campo San Marcuola

Palazzo Vendramin Calergi

Rio della Crea

VeNice

Rio Terà Lista di Spagna

San Marcuola

Grand Canal

Stazione di Santa Lucia (Ferrovia)

APT Office

Ferrovia Scalzi

Palazzo Calbo-Crotta

Riva di Biasio

Rio Terà

Riva de Biasio

San Stae

Disabled-Assistance Office

Ponte dei Scalzi

Campo San Giovanni Decollato

Fond del Megio

C. del Megio

Saliz. Stae

HelloVenezia

HelloVenezia

Clio de Comare

Fond di Santa Lucia

See Santa Croce Map pp100–1

C. Larga

Fond Rimpetto Mocen

Stazione Merci

Ferrovia Santa Lucia

Fond San Simeon Piccolo

Campo San Nazario Sauro

Campo San Giacomo dell'Orio

Piazzale Roma Scomenzera

Piazzale Roma Parisi

Rio Nuovo

Rama Chiavelletta

Ruga Bella o Vecchia San Marina Garzotti

Campo dei Tedeschi

Campo delle Strope

Campo Sant'Agostin

C. Larga

Ponte della Libertà

Ponte di Calatrava

Campo Sant'Agostin

Garage Comunale

Giardini Papadopoli

Fond dei Tolentini

Campiello della Scuola

C. dell'Olio

Campo San Stin

Piazzale Roma

Piazzale Roma Santa Chiara

Corte di Amai

SAN POLO

Campo Tolentini

its bankers, textile merchants and artisans close at hand, and in 1385 allowed Armenian, Jewish, Turkish and Greek communities to reside in Venice proper. Hundreds of Spanish Jews found refuge from the Inquisition here in 1589, but a plaque on the wall recalls the dark days of 5 December 1943 and 17 August 1944, when 289 Venetian Jews were rounded up and deported to Nazi concentration camps. The Jewish retirement home along the northeast side of the square is home to a few survivors. Legend has it that a ghostly rabbi who was spotted in various locations around the square after the WWII deportations mysteriously reappeared in the 1990s. See p19 for more about the Ghetto.

☺ CHIESA DELLA MADONNA DELL'ORTO

Campo della Madonna dell'Orto 3520; admission €2.50, with Chorus pass free; ☽ **10am-5pm Mon-Sat, 1-5pm Sun;** 🚊 **Madonna dell'Orto**
One of Venice's best-kept secrets is this elegantly spare brick Gothic cathedral dedicated to ferrymen, merchants and travellers (hey, that's you), which was the object of Tintoretto's attention (see p15) for decades. No wonder: he lived just over the footbridge from here. Offsetting his stormy *Last Judgment* masterpiece in the apse is his golden-tinged *Presentation*

of the Virgin in the Temple, where an assembly of angels, saints and mere mortals crane their necks to watch her ascend these staggering heights, pointing her out as a shining example to their children. Tintoretto and his family are buried in the corner chapel.

☺ CHIESA DI SANTA MARIA DEI MIRACOLI

☎ **041 2750462; Campo dei Miracoli 6074; admission €2, with Chorus pass free;** ☽ **10am-5pm Mon-Sat, 3-5pm Sun;** 🚊 **Rialto**
There goes the neighbourhood. When Nicolò di Pietro's Madonna icon started miraculously weeping in its outdoor shrine in 1480, crowd control became impossible in this cramped corner of Cannaregio. Out of deference to her holiness – and possibly to disperse foot-traffic jams – the neighbours took up a collection to build a chapel to house the painting and its ecstatic admirers. But there was another miracle in store for the neighbourhood: the church itself. In his design, Pietro Lombardo completely ignored the then popular Gothic style in favour of a simpler, more classical approach that would come to be known as Renaissance architecture. This jewel box of a church is clad inside and out with glistening marble and, in a prime example of Renaissance humanism, Pier Maria Pennacchi filled

each of the 50 wooden ceiling panels with a bright-eyed portrait of a saint or prophet dressed as a Venetian. What started as a modest chapel became a monument to community, and a true icon of Venetian ingenuity.

🟢 MUSEO EBRAICO DI VENEZIA

☎ 041 715359; www.museoebraico.it; **Campo del Ghetto Nuovo 2902b; adult/student €3/2, incl synagogues tour €8/7;** 🕑 **10am-7pm Jun-Sep, 10am-6pm Oct-May;** 🚊 **San Marcuola**
More than a collection of Jewish artefacts, the Museo Ebraico is a starting point for exploring this vibrant Venetian community and its pivotal roles in Venetian arts, architecture, commerce and history. English-language tours take you inside three to five of the seven tiny synagogues in the Ghetto, and leave every half-hour starting at 10.30am. Guided English-language tours of the Antico Cimitero Israelitico (Ancient Jewish Cemetery; p134) convene at 3.30pm on the last Sunday of the month and cost €10. See p19 for more about Venice's Jewish community.

🛍 SHOP
🛍 LUNA *Fashion*
Salizada San Canzian 5917; 🕑 **4-7.30pm Mon, 10am-12.45pm & 4-7.30pm Tue-Sat;** 🚊 **Rialto**

A pebble-print wrap dress, a brown silk shift with matching belt, and a halter dress with a peekaboo neckline may suit different personalities, but they have two things in common: like all of the clothes at Luna, they're designed and made in Italy, and prices are less than what you'd expect for the quality.

🟢 SOLARIS *Books*

☎ 041 5241098; www.libreriasolaris.com; **Rio Terà de la Maddalena 2332;** 🕑 **10am-12.30pm & 4.30-7.30pm Mon-Sat, 4.30-7pm Sun;** 🚊 **San Marcuola**
The plot thickens at Venice's landmark bookstore for comics, mysteries and science fiction. The tiny store is packed with DVDs, books and periodicals, with a back wall that's one big curved bookcase. There's an entire section just for *Corto Maltese,* the graphic novels by Italian comics master Hugo Pratt, the most famous of which are set in Venice.

🍴 EAT
🍴 AL CICHETI *Cicheti*   €

☎ 041 716037; **Calle della Misericordia 367;** 🕑 **7.30am-7.30pm Mon-Fri, 7.30am-1pm Sat;** 🚊 **Ferrovia**
Train or plane food would be a terrible way to end your stay in Venice, so stop by this *bacaro* (bar) near the station to toast your trip with a glass of prosecco and a plate

Rosanna Corró
Paper artisan and designer of book-bound handbags at Carté (p87)

Cosmopolitan paper I started out as a book restorer, and I had access to private collections of ancient books with incredible marbled end papers. The tradition of *carta marmorizzata* [marbled paper] was brought to Venice from Japan via Turkey and Florence, and it evolved every step of the way. When I studied these ancient methods, I saw new possibilities too, things I could bring to the tradition as a Brazilian and Venetian with a modern sensibility. **Cannaregio calm** There's design inspiration right at my doorstep: ancient walls with peeling plaster, the reflection of light on the water, Madonna dell'Orto [p74]. The ratio is about five Venetians for every three tourists, and it's peaceful and sunny along the *fondamente* [canal banks]. **Capturing Venice's mood** No two sheets turn out the same, because each depends on the temperature of the water, the humidity, the mood of that day. If I can capture that moment on paper, I'm happy.

of warming *pasta e ceci* (pasta with chickpeas).

AL FONTEGO DEI PESCATORI
Inventive Venetian €€€

☎ 041 5200538; Calle Priuli 3726;
⌚ noon-3pm & 7-10.30pm Wed-Sun;
🚊 Rialto

Garden dining is the prime option here; it's also the menu inspiration, since chef Bruno takes his wild herbs and local vegetables as seriously as he takes his seafood. Bigoli (a thick type of spaghetti) with cuttlefish and fresh mint, pasta with wild asparagus and clams, and prawn risotto made of wild hops are the seasonal dishes to watch for here, but any dish based on an exotic vegetable or a sea creature you can't pronounce the name of is a good bet.

AL PONTE *Cicheti* €€
☎ 041 5286157; Calle Larga G Gallina 6378; ⌚ 8am-8.30pm Mon-Sat; 🚊 Rialto

A magical combination of luck, early arrival and a Venetian relative will get you a spot at one of the tiny tables at this red-doored pub *al ponte* (on the bridge) but, even if you can't get a table, the *cicheti* (Venetian tapas) here make it worth joining the crowd standing at the bar. Go Fridays for *crudi* (composed bites of raw fish) or any time for baby octopus salad, *panini* (sand-

wiches) with decadently marbled salami, and other seasonal treats.

ALLA VEDOVA
Cicheti, Classic Venetian €

☎ 041 5285324; Calle del Pistor 3912;
⌚ 12.30-3pm & 6.30-10.30pm Mon-Wed, Fri & Sat, 6.30-10.30pm Thu & Sun;
🚊 Ca' d'Oro

Culinary convictions run deep here. Alla Vedova is one of Venice's oldest *osterie*, which is why you won't find *spritz* (a prosecco-based cocktail) or coffee on the menu, and you won't pay more than €1 for a bar snack of Venetian meatballs – and it's best not to get the staff started about spaghetti Bolognese. Enjoy superior seasonal *cicheti* at strictly fair prices at the bar, or call ahead to claim a wood table that has weathered a thousand elbows in postpasta stupors.

ANICE STELLATO *Inventive Venetian, Sustainable Eating* €€€

☎ 041 720744; Fondamenta della Sensa 3272; ⌚ 11am-3pm & 7-11pm Wed-Sun;
🚊 Madonna dell'Orto

The location may seem obscure, but word has gotten out about Anice Stellato's wild sea bass with aromatic herbs and sea salt, its pistachio-encrusted lamb fillet, and its perfectly fried *moeche* (soft-shelled crab). The inspired menu is local and largely organic, with tantalising hints of Venice's

SESTIERI

CANNAREGIO

Organic, friendly, inspired: enjoy a delectable meal at Anice Stellato (p77)

historic spice trade, and the staff proudly serve filtered tap water instead of the environmentally unfriendly bottled stuff. Friendliness is the operative word here, with tables set close enough for chatting, waiters you can trust to choose for you, and prices that are lower than you'd expect for daring cuisine of this calibre.

🍴 ANTICA CANTINA
Classic Venetian €€
☎ 041 7241198; Calle della Testa 6369; 🚤 Rialto
Only a maximum of 20 diners at any given meal can enjoy Antica Cantina's piquant pennette with shrimp, clams and gorgonzola; classic squid in its own ink with buttery grilled polenta; and tangy and surprisingly tender marinated

nervetti (calf's tendons). But if reservations here weren't enough to make a smug foodie out of you, ask about the wine list: most are small-production Veneto wines you can't find for love or money elsewhere, including a white Ca' Rugate uvaggio with extraordinary palate-cleansing properties.

🍴 BEA VITA
Inventive Venetian €€€
☎ 041 2759347; Fondamente delle Cappuccine 3082; 🚤 Guglie
With adventurous specials such as *anatra* (lagoon-duck) risotto drizzled with balsamic reduction and dotted with wild blueberries, the back-room eatery in this local bar is quite a find. Ask your host for wine-pairing suggestions, and you'll be presented with several bottles at a

range of prices from €11 to €40, all of which are solid value.

🍴 DA ALBERTO
Cicheti, Classic Venetian €€

☎ 041 5238153; Calle Larga G Gallina 5401; ⏱ noon-3pm & 6-10pm Mon-Sat; 🚇 Ospedale

This place has all the makings of a true Venetian *osteria* – hidden location, casks of wine, chandeliers that look like medieval torture devices – plus fair prices and a range of seasonal *cicheti* that goes well beyond the usual crostini; dishes include a crispy Venetian seafood fry and salty-sweet *baccalà* (dried cod). Be warned: the kitchen closes early when the joint's not jumping.

🍴 I QUATTRO RUSTEGHI
Classic Venetian €€

☎ 041 715160; www.quattrorusteghi .it/restaurant.htm; Campo del Ghetto Nuovo 2888; 🚇 San Marcuola

Watch the historic Campo del Ghetto Nuovo come alive over a plate of homemade gnocchi, or pasta with zucchini flowers and shrimp, at this pleasant ground-floor eatery under the Scuola Italiana.

🍴 LA CANTINA *Cicheti* €€

☎ 041 5228258; Campo San Felice 3689; 11am-9.30pm Tue-Sat; 🚇 Ca' d'Oro

Damp days are meant for perching on a stool here and warming your face with your bowl of hearty bean soup, while summer scorchers will have you literally over a barrel with a glass of house-brewed Morgana beer and an assortment of bruschette. Food is cooked to order – and slowly at that – so relax and let the world go by.

🍴 VINI DA GIGIO
Classic Venetian €€€

☎ 041 5285140; www.vinidagigio.com; Fondamenta San Felice 3628a; ⏱ 6.30pm-midnight Wed-Sun; 🚇 Ca' d'Oro

Both boats and time drift past this canalside *osteria* without anyone seeming to notice. Must be the scallops served on the half-shell, drizzled with a wine reduction and accompanied by creamy white polenta, or the choice of 'oh, about a thousand' limited-production wines, all personally recommended by your host and resident research scientist of drink, Paolo Lazzari.

🍸 DRINK

🍸 AL TIMON *Cafe-Bar*

☎ 346 3209978; Fondamenta degli Ormesini 2754; ⏱ noon-3pm & 6pm-2am Tue-Sun; 🚇 Guglie

Pull up your director's chair next to the canal and let the show begin. There's a steady parade of been-there-done-that bohemians and starry-eyed students, a massive range of crostini, and enough quality hooch to keep the evening nicely lubricated until the wee hours.

GIRI DI OMBRE: THREE BOOZY VIEWS OF VENICE
Dorsoduro

The quintessential Venetian *giro di ombra* (happy hour) starts at **Cantinone 'Gia Schiavi'** (p122) with an *ombra* (glass) of wine or *pallottoline* (small bottle of beer). Make a pit stop for a mixed plate of cold cuts, marinated veggies and cheese with a glass of house wine at **Osteria alla Bifora** (p123), or head straight onto a *spritz* (prosecco-based cocktail) at **Caffè Rosso** (p122) or **Imagina Café** (p123). By the time you arrive at **ImprontaCafé** (p119), you'll be ready for grilled polenta with mushrooms – and maybe a bracing espresso.

Rialto

This is the perfect *giro di ombra* for lazy drinkers, since all your hooch options are within a couple of blocks. Start at **Osteria I Rusteghi** (p54) for small bar bites served on low courtyard tables with big, full-bodied reds (don't even think about asking for a *spritz* here). Drift over the bridge to **Al Mercà** (p96) for an *ombra* of house wine, then pull up a seat in the piazza to linger over your next glass at **Muro Vino e Cucina** (p96). Finally, roll into **Sacro e Profano** (p96) before the last of the night's speciality pasta is dished out.

Cannaregio

Bar-hop along the waterfront, starting with meatballs and a glass of the good stuff at the bar at **Alla Vedova** (p77). Head onwards and upwards along Rio Terà della Maddalena, through the Ghetto and across the next bridge to **Al Timon** (p79) for some well-earned crostini and a sit-down *ombra* along the canal. Your next move is a tough choice: beer at nearby **Osteria agli Ormesini** (below), or risotto and reasonable wines at handy **Bea Vita** (p78)? Experienced pub crawlers (you know who you are) already know their answer: both.

OSTERIA AGLI ORMESINI
Pub

☎ 041 715834; Fondamenta degli Ormesini 2710; ⏰ 6.30pm-2am Mon-Sat; 🚤 Madonna dell'Orto

While the rest of the city is awash in wine, beer is the drink of choice here, with 120 mostly foreign brews to choose from. The scene inevitably spills into the street, especially when students descend for *panini* – but try to keep it down to a dull roar, or the neighbours and the management get testy.

UN MONDO DI VINO
Wine Bar

☎ 041 5211093; Salizada San Canzian 5984a; ⏰ noon-9pm Tue-Sun; 🚤 Rialto

Get there early to grab the fresh bar nosh – marinated artichokes and mussels, if you're lucky – and a few square inches of ledge to help you balance your plate and glass of wine. There are 45 wines offered by the glass here, and prices range from €1.50 to €3.50, so take a chance on whatever the bartender recommends.

★ PLAY

★ BOTTEGA DEL TINTORETTO
Course

☎ 041 722081; www.tintorettovenezia.it; Fondamenta dei Mori 3400; 5-day course incl lunches & materials €360; ⚓ Rialto

Walking the canals of Cannaregio, you're bound to feel an aquatint coming on – and Roberto Mazzetto can show you how to get that out of your system and onto paper. He runs intensive workshops and five-day summer courses in etching and other forms of printmaking, art and design from the *bottega* (workshop) that was once Tintoretto's studio – not a bad pedigree to bring to your next art project.

★ CASINO DI VENEZIA *Casino*

☎ 041 5297111; www.casinovenezia.it; Campiello Vendramin 2040; admission €5; ⏱ 3pm-2.30am Sun-Thu, 3pm-3am Fri & Sat; ⚓ San Marcuola

Daily dramas at the casino are worthy of their own opera at La Fenice, and that's the way it's been since Venice got the gambling bug in the 16th century. Composer Richard Wagner survived the 20-year effort of writing his stormy

Ring cycle only to die at the casino in 1883. Jackets are required and strong constitutions advisable if you want to take on the tables here – the high stakes are not for the faint of heart.

★ CINEMA GIORGIONE MOVIE D'ESSAI *Cinema*

☎ 041 5226298; Rio Terà di Franceschi 4612; adult/student €7/5; ⏱ shows 5.30pm, 7.30pm & 10pm; ⚓ Ca' d'Oro

This two-screen cinema has a *Cinema Paradiso* feel about it – it's the only cinema in Venice proper, and audiences arrive en masse, primed for entertainment. Spoiler alert: there's an audible buzz of anticipation around any movie with a good review, so if you understand Italian you may hear the ending while waiting to buy tickets.

★ PARADISO PERDUTO
Live Music

☎ 041 720581; Fondamenta della Misericordia 2540; ⏱ 7pm-2am Thu-Mon; ⚓ Madonna dell'Orto

Long tables may make this joint look like a union hall, but it's the right set-up for grog among new friends and for live-music acts that have been known to dissolve into audience-participation jam sessions. Skip the unexceptional food and hit outdoor tables in summer for conversation you can actually hear.

>SAN POLO

Heavenly devotion and earthly delights are neighbours in San Polo, where you'll find both truly divine art and the city's ancient red-light district, now home to artisans' workshops and excellent *osterie* (restaurant-bars). The pride of the *sestiere* (neighbourhood) is a pair of fraternal-twin masterpieces that couldn't be more different: I Frari, with Titian's glowing, gorgeous Madonna; and the Scuola Grande di San Rocco, with its action-packed, turbulent Tintorettos. Foodies can have a different kind of religious experience at the Rialto markets, where mounds of exceptionally fresh seafood and produce look more like offerings to the gods. Photographers elbow drooling gourmets aside to capture glistening fish artfully balanced on their tails atop hillocks of ice, and row after row of exotic vegetables from marshy lagoon gardens. But if it's a retail high you're after, San Polo's artisans' studios will make you think you've died and gone to shopping heaven – without being hell on your wallet.

SAN POLO

⊙ SEE

🏠 SHOP

🍴 EAT

🍷 DRINK

⭐ PLAY

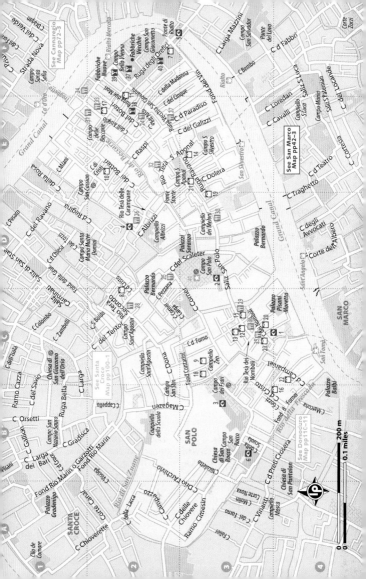

SEE

CASA DI GOLDONI

☎ 041 2759325; www.museiciviciveneziani.it; Calle dei Nomboli 2794; adult/student €2.50/1.50; ⏱ 10am-5pm Mon-Sat Apr-Oct, 10am-4pm Mon-Sat Nov-Mar; 🚢 San Tomà

Comedians, musicians and writers will feel inspiration bubbling up like a belly laugh from the stone floors at the birthplace of Carlo Goldoni (1707–93), creator of *opera buffa* (comic opera) and delicious social satires. As the 1st-floor display explains, Goldoni was a master of second and third acts: he was a doctor's apprentice before switching to law, a back-up career that proved handy when some comedies didn't sell. But Goldoni had the last laugh, with salon sitcoms that made socialites chuckle at themselves. The main draws in the museum are the 18th-century marionettes and puppet theatre, but don't miss chamber-music concerts held here; see the museum's website for a schedule.

CHIESA DI SAN POLO

Campo San Polo 2118; admission €3, with Chorus pass free; ⏱ 10am-5pm Mon-Sat; 🚢 San Silvestro

This 9th-century Byzantine church has kept a low profile over the centuries while housing grew up around it, so most travellers speed past without realising it's there. With a high ship's-keel ceiling and stained-glass windows from the 14th to 15th centuries, San Polo is surprisingly airy inside, if a little dark – and the same is true of the art. Tintoretto's *Last Supper* is rife with tension, as apostles react with outrage, hurt and anger at Jesus' news that one of them will betray him. Giandominico Tiepolo (son of baroque ceiling maestro Giambattista) shows the dark side of humanity in his *Stations of the Cross:* jeering onlookers torment Jesus, his blood-stained rags contrasting with their baroque finery. Literally and figuratively, Tiepolo lays it on thickly, so that when a lushly painted Jesus leaps from his tomb on the gold ceiling, it's the ultimate comeuppance for his tormentors.

I FRARI

Chiesa di Santa Maria Gloriosa dei Frari; Campo dei Frari; admission €3, with Chorus pass free; ⏱ 9am-6pm Mon-Sat, 1-6pm Sun; 🚢 San Tomà

Is it hot in here, or is it just Titian's 1518 *Madonna of the Assumption* (see p16)? This smouldering altar masterpiece draws visitors into the apse and out of this world, capturing the moment the Madonna escapes this mortal coil and reaches heavenward, her signature Titian red robe in glorious disarray as she finds her footing on a cloud. Inside the painting, on-

SESTIERI

SAN POLO

Feel your jaw drop (multiple times) at glorious I Frari

lookers below gasp and point out the ascending Madonna to one another – not unlike the modern-day visitors to the church. As if this weren't already too much to handle, the lofty Gothic brick church has other wow-factor features: minuscule puzzlework marquetry in the *coro* (choir stalls), Giovanni Bellini's achingly sweet sacristy triptych, Titian's *Madonna di Ca' Pesaro* to the left of the choir, and the marble-pyramid mausoleum of Antonio Canova, which the artist had originally intended as a monument to Titian. Titian was lost to the plague aged 90 in 1576, but legend has it that, in light of his contribution to I Frari, the strict rules of quarantine were bent to allow his burial in the church.

PONTE DELLE TETTE
Rialto

'Tits Bridge' got its name in the late 15th century, when neighbourhood prostitutes were encouraged to display their wares in the windows instead of taking their marketing campaigns to the streets. Crossing over the bridge, you'll reach Rio Terà delle Carampane, named after the house of a noble family (Ca' Rampani) that became notorious as a meeting place for local working girls, who to this day are known as *carampane*.

🄲 PONTE DI RIALTO
🄻 **Rialto**

An amazing feat of engineering in its day, Antonio da Ponte's 1592 marble bridge was for centuries the only land link across the Grand Canal. The construction cost 250,000 gold ducats, a staggering sum that puts cost overruns for the new Ponte di Calatrava (p102) into perspective. Now that the Rialto is clogged with kiosks and foot-traffic jams, locals go out of their way to avoid it, or zip up the less scenic northern side of the bridge. The southern side faces San Marco and, after the crowds of shutterbugs and tour groups clear out around sunset, it offers panoramas of a picturesque stretch of the Grand Canal lined with *palazzi* (palaces or mansions).

🄲 SCUOLA GRANDE DI SAN ROCCO
☎ **041 5234864; www.scuolagrande sanrocco.it; Campo San Rocco 3052; adult/under 26yr €7/5;** ⏱ **9am-5.30pm Apr-Oct, 10am-5pm Nov-Mar;** 🄻 **San Tomà**

Tintoretto's masterpiece took 23 years to complete (1575–87), but it's so fresh and immediate you'd swear the paint is still wet. Everyone wanted the commission to paint this building, dedicated to the patron saint of the plague stricken, so Tintoretto had to produce something exceptional – and, just to be sure he won, he cheated a little. Instead of producing sketches like his rival Paolo Veronese, Tintoretto painted a ceiling piece and dedicated it to the saint – knowing the confraternity couldn't refuse an offering to San Rocco, and that other painters would have to work around the piece. Tintoretto went all out in the upstairs Sala Grande Superiore, covering the walls with action-packed biblical scenes that read like a graphic novel. This painting cycle seems to come with its own sound effects: you can almost hear the *swoop!* overhead as an angel dives down to feed an ailing Elijah. Unlike the Venetian colourists, Tintoretto concentrated on dynamic lines, and you can see the roots of modern abstract expressionism in *Agony in the Garden*, where a sketchy, anxious Jesus hides his fate against a black, X-shaped void. See p15 for more on Tintoretto.

🛍 SHOP
🄲 **ATTOMBRI** *Jewellery*
☎ **041 5212524; www.attombri.com; Sotoportego Orafi 74, Rialto;** ⏱ **9am-1pm & 3-7pm Mon-Sat;** 🄻 **Rialto**

Dolce&Gabbana models recently worked Attombri designs on Milan catwalks; now you too can strut the Rialto in this dramatic, handcrafted jewellery. Stefano and Daniele

Attombri bend wire into waves, which then curl around the wrist with lagoon green beads, or grace the collarbone with red-beaded starfish. Prices start at around €40, making these accessories a steal compared to a D&G tee.

BOTTEGA DEGLI ANGELI
Ceramics

☎ 041 710866; www.bottegangeli.com; Calle del Cristo 2224; ⏰ 10am-1pm & 3-8pm Mon-Sat; 🚊 Rialto

Huge vases, smallish tiles, tiny pendants: there's something to suit every taste and carry-on limit here. The work of the three resident ceramists ranges from stark, dramatic shapes to abstract stained-glass patterns and even whimsical fish, but the signature is a bright red glaze that (as any ceramist will tell you) is quite difficult to achieve. Wish you could do that? Try your hand at the pottery wheel at upcoming workshops and classes.

CAMPIELLO CA' ZEN
Antiques

☎ 041 714871; www.campiellocazen .com; Campiello Zen 2581; ⏰ 9am-1pm & 3-7pm Mon-Sat; 🚊 San Tomà

An antique glass lamp would be the last thing you'd want to cram in your luggage – or so you thought before you saw the 1940s Salviati silvery bluebell chandelier and the ultramod Scarpa table lamps.

That fabulous hand-blown chalice seems downright practical by comparison. But here's a dangerous thought: Campiello Ca' Zen ships.

CARTE *Paper Crafts*

☎ 320 0248776; Calle di Cristi 1731; ⏰ 9am-1pm & 3-7.30pm Mon-Sat; 🚊 San Tomà

Paperwork never seemed such a good idea. After years of restoring ancient manuscripts and books, Rosanna Corró (p76) decided to put those skills to work making something entirely original, and she's been on a roll ever since. This tiny shop is packed with must-have paper-and-clothbound purses in lagoon-ripple patterns; peacock-eye marbled paper panels that bring Venetian glamour to your living room walls; swirly op-art jewellery boxes that outshine their contents; and marbled wood-grain albums and journals that will do justice to your Venice trip.

DROGHERIA MASCARI
Food, Wine

☎ 041 5229762; Ruga degli Spezieri 381; ⏰ 8am-1pm & 4-7.30pm Mon, Tue & Thu-Sat, 8am-1pm Wed; 🚊 San Silvestro

Food is the drug of choice at this historic spice merchant, where wares are still dispensed from banks of tiny wooden drawers and copper-topped jars. Window

Feed your imagination at Drogheria Mascari (p87)

displays feature ziggurat-shaped piles of cayenne and leaning towers of star anise alongside bio-dynamic Veneto wines and estate-grown olive oils. For an impressive selection of Italian wines starting at €5.50, don't miss the *enoteca* (wine bar) out the back.

FANNY *Leather Goods*
☎ 041 5228266; Calle dei Saoneri 2723; ⏰ 10am-7.30pm; 🚏 San Tomà
Quit snickering about the name – when that Venice chill hits your extremities, you'll be seriously glad you found this treasure trove of leather gloves. No need to sacrifice style for warmth here: check out the purple pair with tiny yellow

buttons, or those cashmere-lined turquoise numbers. At these prices, splashy orange wrist-strap clutches and spring green leather handbags are tempting add-on sales.

GILBERTO PENZO *Model Boats*
☎ 041 719372; Calle 2 dei Saoneri 2681; ⏰ 9am-12.30pm & 3-6pm Mon-Sat; 🚏 San Tomà
Yes, you actually can take a gondola home in your pocket. Anyone fascinated by the models at the Museo Storico Navale (p62) will go wild here amid handmade wooden models of all kinds of Venetian boats, including some that are seaworthy (or, at least, bathworthy). For crafty types, Signore Penzo creates kits so you can have a crack at it yourself.

HIBISCUS *Fashion*
☎ 041 5208989; Ruga Rialto 1060; 10am-6.30pm; 🚏 San Silvestro
Caught in Venice without a stitch to wear to a Biennale opening? You can either hope for a fairy godmother or head straight to Hibiscus. Venice's creative cross-roads style is built here piece by distinctive piece: a flowing Italian dress ruched at the bottom for impact, a Japanese jacket with inbuilt flaps in water-resistant canvas, and a locally made ceramic-disc necklace.

🏛 I VETRI A LUME DI AMADI
Glass

☎ 041 5238089; Calle Saoneri 2747;
🕐 9am-12.30pm & 3-6pm Mon-Sat;
🚇 San Silvestro

Glass menageries don't get more fascinating than the one created before your eyes by Signore Amadi. Sea anemones with glowing pink-tipped tentacles and fierce little glass crabs waving their claws are just the beginning of the wonders here: check out the medicine cabinet display of eerily lifelike glass mosquitoes, balancing on spindly legs the width of a hair. The remarkable blue glass horses look like Picasso drawings in three dimensions, and the glass beans and spring onions may leave you craving vegetables for lunch.

🏛 IL BAULE BLU *Antiques, Toys*

☎ 041 719448; San Tomà 2915a;
🕐 10.30am-12.30pm & 4-7.30pm Mon-Sat;
🚇 San Tomà

On recent inspection, this curiosity cabinet of elusive treasures included antique Steiff teddy bears, vintage Murano *murrine* (glass beads), a pale pink silk Jil Sander suit and a cigar box of Bakelite buttons. If travel has proved tough on your kid's favourite toy, first aid and kind words will be administered at the in-house teddy hospital.

🏛 IL GUFO ARTIGIANO
Leather Goods

☎ 041 5234030; Ruga del Speziali 299;
🕐 10am-1pm & 3-7pm Mon-Sat;
🚇 Rialto

Venice pictures demand a suitable album, and here you can have your pick of leather ones embossed by hand in glowing colours made with vegetable dyes. The swirling designs – which are also embossed onto journals, handbags and wallets – come from ironwork on Venetian windows, but are combined with abstract modern flair.

🏛 LA BOTTEGA DI GIO
Jewellery

☎ 041 714664; Fondamenta dei Frari 2559a; 🕐 10am-1pm & 3-7pm Mon-Sat;
🚇 San Tomà

The glass necklaces in the shops not quite your style? Make your own with genuine Murano glass beads and your choice of coloured wire, silk thread or leather cord at this DIY jewellery shop. Lampwork beads begin at €1, and one or two may be all you need for a highly original Venice souvenir.

🏛 MILLE E UNA NOTA
Musical Instruments

☎ 041 5231822; Calle di Mezzo 1235;
🕐 9.45am-1pm & 3.30-7.30pm Mon-Sat;
🚇 San Tomà

The same thought occurs to almost everyone after hearing

Stunning handmade paper in multiple styles and colours? It's enough to make you lose your marbles

Interpreti Veneziani (p97): is it too late to take up an instrument? The easiest option would be the harmonica, and Mille e Una Note has an impressive range of vintage and modern ones from the Italian Alps and Switzerland. But, if you're feeling very ambitious, you can pick up some Albinoni sheet music and a lute here too.

SABBIE E NEBBIE
Gifts, Homewares
☎ 041 719073; Calle dei Nomboli 2768a; ⏱ 10am-12.30pm & 4-7.30pm Mon-Sat; ⛴ San Tomà

The latest East–West trade-route trends begin here, with Japanese-inspired Rina Menardi ceramics,

woven opera wraps made in India and handmade books from Bologna created with Japanese paper-marbling techniques.

SERENA VIANELLO *Fashion*
☎ 041 5223351; www.serenavianello.com; Campo San Aponal 1226; ⏱ 10am-noon & 3.30-7.30pm Mon-Sat; ⛴ San Tomà

Opulent Como silks and minute finishings set these timeless Venetian designs apart from the faddish crowd. Two-tone silk handbags apply Tiepolo colour schemes in sky blues and golds, while a silk jacket evokes a walk through Venice, with gossamer green tones and aubergine architectural details.

SESTIERI

SAN POLO

🏠 VIZIO VIRTÙ Food
☎ 041 2750149; www.viziovirtu.com;
Calle de Campaniel 2829a; ⌚ 10am-
6.30pm Mon-Sat; 🚊 San Tomà
Work your way through Venice's
most decadent vices and tasty virtues at this extraordinary chocolate shop. As if the hot-chocolate
fountain weren't enough of a Willy
Wonka–esque attraction, the filled
chocolates here come in a five-
course meal of flavours: blueberry
and violet, barolo wine, redcurrant
and basil, balsamic vinegar, and
'Freud' (which tastes like a cigar,
naturally).

👗 ZAZU Fashion
☎ 041 715426; Calle dei Saoneri 2750;
⌚ 2.30-7.30pm Mon, 9.30am-1.30pm &
2.30-7.30pm Tue-Sat; 🚊 San Tomà
Be the fashion world's Ms Marco
Polo with your Italian-designed
tapestry bags, one-of-a-kind dresses from Barcelona and Japanese
wrap tops. Prices are above sports-
wear but below couture, and the
sale rack in the back usually has
great pieces for €50 to €100.

🍴 EAT
🍴 ALL'ARCO Cicheti €€
☎ 041 5205666; Calle dell'Arco 436;
⌚ 7am-5pm Mon-Sat; 🚊 San Silvestro
'I want what she's having…' is
always the right order at All'Arco,
where the best cicheti (Venetian

tapas) in town aren't on the menu,
and technically don't even have
a name. Maestro Francesco (see
p93) and his son Matteo make
them up daily, with Francesco
commandeering the kitchen's
tiny burners to turn out one of his
'fantasias' of grilled prawns with
white asparagus tips wrapped in
pancetta and sage, while Matteo
takes over after Saturday fish
deliveries to invent a tuna tartare
with mint, strawberries and a
balsamic reduction. Even with co-
pious prosecco, hardly any meal
devoured at the bar ever tops €20
or falls short of four stars – you
might as well book your return
ticket to Venice now.

🍴 ANTICA BIRRERIA LA
CORTE Pizza €€
☎ 041 2750570; Campo San Polo 2168;
⌚ noon-11pm; 🚊 San Silvestro
This former bullfight pen became
a brewery in the 19th century to
keep Venice's Austrian occupiers
occupied, and now it's a modern
eatery featuring (you guessed it)
grilled beef and good beer. Pizza
is the way to go here, including
such nontouristy versions as
rocket, bresaola (air-dried beef)
and grana padano. With room for
150, there's hardly ever a wait,
and the piazza seating is perfect
for outdoor movie screenings
and live-theatre performances in
summer.

🍴 ANTICHE CARAMPANE
Classic Venetian €€€

☎ 041 5240165; www.antichecaram
pane.com; Rio Terà delle Carampane
1911; ⏱ Tue-Sat; 🚊 San Stae

Hidden in the former red-light
district behind Ponte delle
Tette (Tits Bridge), this culinary
indulgence is a bit of a trick to
find. Cheap it's not, and you may
wonder who you have to, erm,
know to get a reservation, but
the home cooking, the intimate
atmosphere and the sign proudly
announcing No Tourist Menu are
a welcome change from bog-
standard options of pizza or pasta
Bolognese.

🍴 DAI ZEMEI *Cicheti* €

☎ 041 5208546; www.ostariadaizemei
.it; Ruga Vecchia San Giovanni 1045;
⏱ 9am-8pm; 🚊 San Silvestro

The twins (*zemei*) who run this
corner joint are a blur of mo-
tion by 10am, preparing for the
onslaught of regulars and the odd
well-informed foodie tourist. The
toasted bruschette are usually
the first to go along with the lard-
and-rocket *panini* (sandwiches),
but there's always a good range
of crostini, including gorgonzola with walnuts and a brandy
reduction. Think past the usual
prosecco and wash it down with
a rustic raboso or sophisticated
refosco.

🍴 MAJER GELATERIA &
ENOTECA *Gelato, Wine Bar* €

☎ 041 722873; www.majer.it; Calle del
Scalater 2307; ⏱ 11am-9pm; 🚊 Riva
di Biasio

Venetian parents chilling out
on benches while their kids tear
around Campo San Polo share a little secret: this *gelateria* (ice-cream
shop) is adjacent to a wine-tasting
room. While the kiddies are occupied with an outstanding *frutti di
bosco* (wild berry) gelato, you can
nip next door for a tipple, which is
charged by the *ombra* (glass) with
a prepaid €5 card.

🍴 OSTERIA LA PATATINA AL
PONTE
Cicheti, Classic Venetian €€

☎ 041 5237238; www.lapatatina.it;
Calle dei Saoneri 2741a; ⏱ 6-10pm
Mon, 9.30am-2.30pm & 6-10pm Tue-Sat;
🚊 San Tomà

Some preparation is required to
get the right *piatta mista* (mixed
plate) here, so head up to the
counter and ask for tasting portions of whatever looks fresh and
tasty. Classic bets are *baccalà con
polenta* (cod with polenta), *griglia
mista* (grilled vegetables) and
bigoli in salsa (thick spaghetti in
tomato, anchovy and onion sauce).
The deep-fried *tramezzini* (sandwiches) are tasty, but are challeng-
ing to digest, even with assistance
from the house prosecco.

Francesco Pinto
Maestro of cicheti (Venetian tapas) at All'Arco (p91) and third-generation osteria (restaurant-bar) impresario

Why there's no menu It's like Venice: there are some common themes and ingredients, but the rest is pure fantasy, and what you find today might not be here tomorrow. I'm more of a traditionalist, but my son Matteo makes modern dishes, Italian *crudi* [composed bites of raw fish] with a creative touch like a sushi chef. Cooking isn't work, it's something we do for fun.

Don't leave Venice without tasting…*Sarde in saor* [sardines in an onion marinade] and *baccalà mantecato* [mashed cod prepared in garlic and parsley], not made industrially but with dried cod that is soaked for 48 hours. Try ancient Venetian dishes like *nervetti* [calf's tendons] and *trippa* [tripe]… *[interrupts himself]* Do you smell that? Somebody's cooking squid. *Seppioline in nero* [squid cooked in its own ink], you must try that…you'd better stay awhile. **How to thank the cook** Just come and eat well. Stay an hour, give us time to invent some new dish for you. That's gratification enough.

SESTIERI

SAN POLO

🍴 PASTICCERIA RIZZARDINI
Pastries €
☎ 041 5223835; Campiello dei Meloni 1415; ⏱ 7.30am-8pm Wed-Mon; 🚏 San Silvestro

'From 1742' reads the modest storefront sign, and inside you'll find the secret weapons that have helped this little bakery last so long: killer cream puffs and dangerous doughnuts. Trawl the biscuit section in search of wagging *lingue di suocere* (mother-in-law's tongues), *pallone di Casanova* (Casanova's balls) and other *dolci tipici Venexiani* (typical Venetian sweets), but act fast if you want that last slice of tiramisu.

🍴 PESCHERIA *Self-Catering*
Rialto; ⏱ 7am-2pm; 🚏 Rialto

Slinging fresh fish daily for 700 years and still going strong, the fishmongers here are more vital to Venetian cuisine than any chef. Ask how and where a seafood delicacy was caught, and you'll get an earful about recent shifts in Adriatic aquaculture. Sustainable fishing is not new here: marble plaques show regulations set centuries ago for minimum allowable sizes for various types of fish. See also p14.

🍴 PIZZERIA ANTICO PANIFICIO *Bakery, Pizza*
€
Campiello del Sol 929; ⏱ bakery noon-3pm & 7-11pm Thu-Mon, restaurant noon-3pm & 7-11pm Wed-Mon; 🚏 San Silvestro

Most Venetian pizzerias pander to tourists, but this spot is a local institution. Outdoor seating is always packed, so be prepared to lunge at free tables and order decisively. Basic choices such as margherita (with basil, mozzarella and tomato) insult the chef's intelligence – go with anchovies, zucchini flowers or whatever topping your neighbours are enjoying.

🍴 PRONTO PESCE PRONTO
Cicheti €€
☎ 041 8220298; Pescheria, Rialto 319; ⏱ 9am-3.30pm & 5-7.30pm; 🚏 Rialto

The fish at the Pescheria (left) look so good you might want to eat them raw – and you can do just that at this fish store that prepares delightful *crudi* (composed bites of raw fish) and lightly dressed seafood salads. There's a counter for leaning on and prosecco for washing it down but, to bump your lunch up a star, take that *folpeti* (baby-octopus) salad and naturally sweet raw-prawn *crudi* down to the dock by the Grand Canal.

🍴 RIALTO PRODUCE MARKETS *Self-Catering*
Rialto; ⏱ 7am-3.30pm; 🚏 Rialto

Getting your daily servings of fruit and veg is easy here – you'll be tempted by tantalising teetering pyramids of colourful produce.

DIY DINNERS: SOME ASSEMBLY REQUIRED

When nothing on the menu seems to hit the mark, you can always assemble a meal to your liking in Venice's markets. If you missed the **Rialto produce markets** (p14, opposite) in full swing in the morning, stop by the **floating farmers market** (Map pp110–11, D3; Campo San Barnaba, Dorsoduro), docked alongside Campo San Barnaba. A warning, though: the produce-barge vendor is a grumpy character who sometimes insists on 500g minimum purchases, knowing you won't be able to resist those piles of tomatoes and blood oranges. Nearby is the **Dorsoduro produce market** (Map pp110–11, D2; Campo Santa Margherita, Dorsoduro), where during the week you'll spot vegetable and fruit stalls, and a small, cheerful fish market oozing squid ink onto the flagstones. If takeaway is more your style, head for the deli counter and bakery at **Coop** (p104), or to **Pronto Pesce Pronto** (opposite) for seafood dishes to go. For something to wash it all down, bring your empty water bottle and fill 'er up straight from the barrel at **Nave d'Oro** (8.30am-1pm & 4.30-7.30pm Mon, Tue, Thu-Sat), the wine dispensary with locations in Cannaregio (Map pp72–3, D4, F5), Castello (Map pp60–1, A2, B2) and Dorsoduro (Map pp110–11, D2).

Now the question is 'Where to eat?' Picnicking in Venetian piazzas and *calli* (streets) is forbidden, but you can head to the beaches on the **Lido** (p134), the gardens at the **Biennale pavilions** (p59), the courtyard at your B&B or hostel, or your hotel balcony overlooking the Grand Canal (lucky you) for lunch with a Venetian view.

Salad cravings are a given when you're surrounded by juicy tomatoes, aromatic greens and, in season, tender *castraure* (baby artichokes). Vendors are used to visitors looking and photographing rather than buying, but if you're in the market for picnic makings they might offer you samples. See also p14.

🍴 SNACK BAR AI NOMBOLI
Sandwiches €

☎ 041 5230995; Rio Terà dei Nomboli 271c; ☻ 8am-8pm Mon-Sat; 🚢 San Tomà

This snappy Venetian comeback to McDonald's has scrumptious

crusty rolls filled with local cheeses; savoury salami, prosciutto, roast beef and other cold cuts; roast vegetables and sprightly greens that are more than garnishes; and condiments ranging from spicy mustard to wild-nettle sauce. Two sandwiches is a filling lunch; three is a proper feast.

🍴 TRATTORIA DA IGNAZIO
Classic Venetian €€

☎ 041 5234852; Calle Saoneri 2749; ☻ noon-3pm & 7-11pm Mon-Sat; 🚢 San Silvestro

Old-school charm is the key here: grilled lagoon fish and homemade pasta ('of course') are served with a proud flourish by dapper, well-fed waiters, who know they're providing good quality at a fair price. The cheerful dining room with yellow linens and orchids on every table is pretty enough, but on sunny days and warm nights the entire neighbourhood converges beneath the grape arbour in the garden.

DRINK

AL MERCÀ *Wine Bar*

Campo Bella Vienna 213; noon-3pm & 5-9pm Mon-Sat; Rialto

The night is young and so is Al Mercà's clientele, who nurse wine or beer as they catch up with old friends they haven't seen since this time yesterday and scrap dinner plans in favour of *cicheti*. Wine by the glass ranges from €2 to €3.50, and *cicheti* start at just €1 for meatballs and mini *panini*. Arrive by 6.30pm for the best selection and easy bar access, or you'll constantly be repeating '*permesso*' (pardon) as you squeeze through the spillover crowd in the piazza.

DO MORI *Wine Bar*

☎ 041 5225401; Sotoportego dei do Mori 429; 8.30am-8pm Mon-Sat; Rialto

Behind the kiosk-strewn tourist thoroughfare to the Rialto lurks this sultry backstreet beauty from another era, with its gleaming,

gargantuan copper pots and incongruously dainty sandwiches called *francobolli* (literally 'postage stamps'). Come early for the best selection of *cicheti* and local gossip.

MURO VINO E CUCINA
Cocktail Bar, Wine Bar

☎ 041 5237495; Campo Bella Vienna 222; 4pm-1am Mon-Sat; Rialto

There's no velvet rope here, though it's the kind of place you'd expect to find one, given the aluminium bar, sexy lighting and see-and-be-seen picture windows. But the prices are still refreshingly friendly, with wines by the glass starting at €2 and respectable cocktails from €5. The upstairs restaurant may be pricier, but the place to be here is by the bar for *cicheti* or at a low table out in the square for late-night drinks.

SACRO E PROFANO *Wine Bar*

☎ 041 5237924; Ramo Terzo del Parangon 502; 7pm-1am Thu-Tue; Rialto

Musicians, artists, esoteric philosophers and the odd nutter make the crowd at this hideaway under the Rialto exceptionally fun to be around – you never know who's going to burst out into a rhyme or rant next. Once you're drawn into conversation, you'll wind up settling in for a generous plate of pasta, witnessing an impromptu poetry recital and getting invited along to a ska show.

⭐ PLAY

⭐ INTERPRETI VENEZIANI
Classical Music

☎ 041 2770561; www.interpreti veneziani.com; Scuola Grande di San Rocco, Campo San Rocco 3052; adult/ student & senior €24/19; 🕑 doors open 8.30pm; 🚊 San Tomà

Everything you knew of Vivaldi from elevators and telephone hold music turns out to be fantastically wrong. Interpreti Veneziani play Vivaldi as a soundtrack for this city of intrigue, and you'll never listen to *The Four Seasons* again without hearing summer storms gathering over the lagoon and the echo of hurried footsteps over bridges in a winter's night intrigue. Soloists strike resonating chords and pull startling vibrations from original 18th-century instruments, adding new urgency to classical music. Some rare spliced gene is the only way to explain the talents and showmanship of the Amadio family (see p129), three of whom are part of the ensemble, which performs Vivaldi nightly in the Scuola Grande di San Rocco (p86) as though it was experiencing

Interpreti Veneziani tops the bill in Venice

every emotion of every movement for the first time. See p23 for more on baroque music.

⭐ SUMMER ARENA
Cinema, Theatre

Campo San Polo; 🕑 Jul-Aug; 🚊 San Tomà

In summer ancient Campo San Polo becomes the forward-thinking Summer Arena, with free open-air cinema, concerts and theatre performances. This space is wide open to ideas year-round, however, so watch out for political rallies and impromptu rave sessions.

>SANTA CROCE

So this is how Venice lives when it's not busy entertaining. Santa Croce is a network of winding lanes lined with artisans' studios, *campi* (squares) where kids tear around on tricycles while adults sip prosecco, pizza joints that are cheap enough for teenagers on dates, alternative-culture outposts and (since this is Venice, after all) a couple of charmingly quirky museums in historic *palazzi* (palaces or mansions). When the Rialto scene gets too overwhelming, wander west through Santa Croce past Byzantine churches and baroque houses, stopping frequently for outstanding gelato (perennial local favourite: pistachio). Beyond the museums and a couple of churches, there's not much here of major tourist interest, which is what makes it an ideal place to really unwind. No traffic or souvenir salespeople here; instead, there's just the murmur of idle chatter in backstreet *bacari* (restaurant-bars), water lapping at the canal banks, and unhurried footsteps along single-file *calle* (streets).

SANTA CROCE

Please see over for map

◉ SEE

◉ CA' PESARO

☎ 041 721127; www.museiciviciven eziani.it; Fondamenta di Ca' Pesaro 2076; adult/EU 6-14yr, student & over 65yr €5.50/3; ☷ 10am-6pm Tue-Sun Apr-Oct, 10am-5pm Tue-Sun Nov-Mar; ⛴ San Stae

This highly eccentric museum is really a three-in-one special: modern art plus Japanese antiques, all in a 1710 Baldassare Longhena–designed *palazzo*. The ground-floor Galleria d'Arte Moderna begins with the shamelessly self-promoting early days of the Biennale, and its emphasis on Venetian landscapes, Venetian painters (notably Giacomo Favretto) and socialites who supposedly embodied mythological virtues. But the savvy Biennale foundation bought key works shown in other national pavilions too – notably Gustav Klimt's 1909 *Judith II (Salome)* and Marc Chagall's *Rabbi of Vitebsk* (1914–22). The Pesaro family commissioned the 1901 portrait of grande dame Letizia from future futurist Giacomo Balla, while the De Lisi bequest in 1961 added Kandinskys and Morandis to the mix. Upstairs is the wonderfully quirky Museo Orientale, the result of an 1887–9 shopping spree

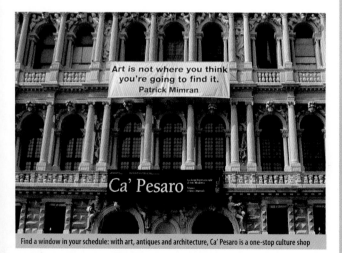

Find a window in your schedule: with art, antiques and architecture, Ca' Pesaro is a one-stop culture shop

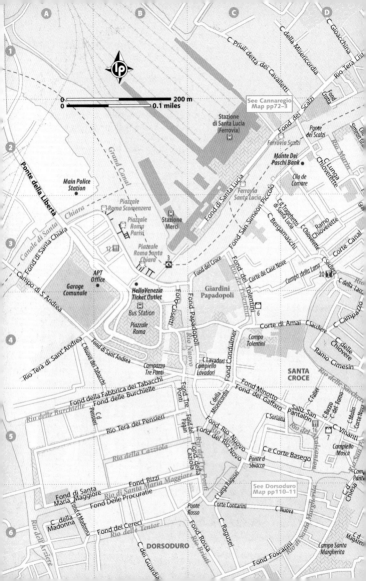

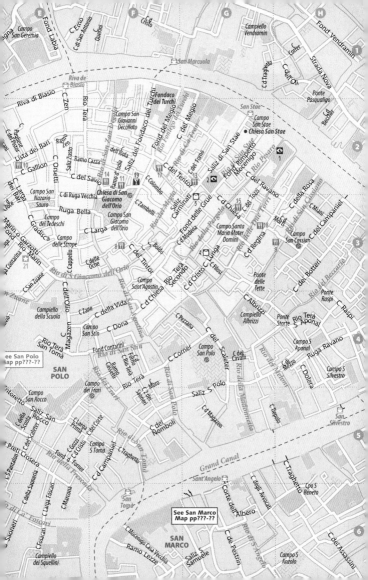

A black-and-red colour scheme never dates

Fashionistas and fans of costume drama shouldn't miss this museum of textiles, housed in the swanky 18th-century salons of a Gothic Grand Canal palace. It's easy to imagine romance blossoming under the ceiling fresco in the green drawing room, and elections of the doge (Venice's leader) being negotiated in the count's library – seven Mocenigo family members served as dogi. Each room features appropriate garments: a lethal-looking corset in the contessa's bedroom, English-influenced damask rose gowns with plunging necklines in the red living room, and deep red procurators' robes that hid expanding waistlines in the dining room.

across Asia by Prince Enricodi Borbone. He reached Japan when Edo art was being discounted in favour of modern Meiji, and his Edo-era swords, *netsukes* (miniature sculptures), musical instruments and lacquerware writing sets are highlights of this collection of 30,000 objets d'art.

⊙ PALAZZO MOCENIGO
☎ 041 721798; www.museicivicivenez iani.it; Salizada di San Stae 1992; adult/ EU 6-14yr, student & over 65yr €4/2.50; ☼ 10am-5pm Tue-Sun Apr-Oct, 10am-4pm Tue-Sun Nov-Mar; ⛴ San Stae

⊙ PONTE DI CALATRAVA
⛴ Ferrovia, Piazzale Roma
Although it had only just opened when this book went to print, the Calatrava Bridge has already been called many things: a fish tail, a fantasy, unnecessary, overdue, pleasingly streamlined and displeasingly wheelchair inaccessible. There are, however, two things that everyone agrees on: it was expensive and it was late. Budgeted at around €4 million in 2001, the cost of the bridge trebled as engineers corrected a 4cm tolerance that raised questions about its stability. Decide for yourself if the

time and money paid off – then join the ongoing debates at happy hour across Venice.

🛒 SHOP

🏠 CARTAVENEZIA *Paper Crafts*

☎ 041 5241283; Calle Lunga 2125; ⌚ 3.30-7.30pm Mon, 11am-1pm & 3.30-7.30pm Tue-Sat; 🚊 San Stae

Paper is really put through the wringer here – but instead of marbling it, as has been the custom in Venice for about 150 years, CartaVenezia embosses and sculpts its handmade cotton paper. Ancient techniques meet modern industrial chic in the striped raw-edged bowls and lampshades, moulded-paper jewellery embellished with steel, and abstract friezes that demand prime placement in urban lofts.

🏠 EL CANAPON *Fashion, Gifts*

☎ 041 2440247; Salizada de San Stae 1906; 🚊 San Stae

Alternative culture pops up in the weirdest places in Venice, and El Canapon is exhibit A. Satisfy munchies across the street at the *gelateria,* then shop here for hemp clothing that's actually stylish, and for psychedelically swirled shoulder bags that are just right for DJs transporting trip-hop albums to a gig. Staff will gladly fill you in on upcoming shows and protests.

🏠 MAREDICARTA *Books, Boating Aids*

☎ 041 716304; www.maredicarta.com; Fondamenta dei Tolentini; ⌚ 9am-1pm & 3.30-7.30pm Mon-Sat; 🚊 Ferrovia

Sailors and armchair seafarers will geek out with utter glee at this store, which is packed with every map and DIY aid you could possibly need for lagoon exploration, boat upkeep and spotting local sealife. If you're considering rowing lessons or a boat purchase – and who doesn't after a few days on the lagoon? – stop here first and get informed; you can also pick up a schedule of boating classes offered through the store.

🏠 PENNY LANE VINTAGE *Fashion, Sustainable Shopping*

☎ 041 5244134; www.pennylane vintage.com; Salizada San Pantalon; ⌚ 9.30am-8.30pm Mon-Sat; 🚊 Ferrovia

If oversized Italian 1960s shades are more your style than Carnevale masks, Penny Lane has you covered. Inspiration comes equally from vintage Venice and swinging '60s London, from the *Yellow Submarine* decor and Ben Sherman shirts to mod yellow macs with white piping and skintight nautical striped sweaters. Vintage-inspired new clothing is displayed up front, but the back area has the major vintage steals – €10 for that mac and €5 for a striped men's sweater circa 1970.

☞ EAT

☞ AE OCHE Pizza €
☎ 041 5241161; www.aeoche.com; Calle del Tintor 1552a; ☿ noon-2.20pm & 7-10.30pm Mon-Fri, noon-2.20pm & 7-11.30pm Sat & Sun; ⚓ San Stae
Champ Louisiana sweet potatoes and Long-Distance Sodas are advertised on vintage signs here, but both the crowd and the 70-pizza menu are modern Venetian. Daredevils order the *equino* (horse meat with lemon) or *mangiafuoco* ('fire-eater'; hot salami, capsicum and tabasco), but perennial favourites are the *tonnata* (tuna, capers and onions) and *estiva* (rocket, seasoned grana padano and cherry tomatoes).

☞ AL NONO RISORTO
Classic Venetian, Pizza €€
☎ 041 5241169; Sotoportego de Siora Bettina 2338; ☿ noon-3pm & 6-10pm Thu-Tue; ⚓ San Stae
Manifesto or menu? At Al Nono Risorto, pizzas are listed alongside urgent action alerts: 'No abandoning animals! More rights for gays and domestic partners!' Prices are left of centre, radical-chic servers can't be bothered with petty bourgeois orders and, on sunny days, all of Venice converges on the garden for squid with polenta,

bargain house prosecco and political bonding.

☞ ALASKA GELATERIA
Gelato, Sustainable Eating €
☎ 041 715211; Calle Larga dei Bari 1159; ☿ 9am-1pm & 3-8pm; ⚓ Riva de Biasio
Kids may like their ice cream blue and with gum balls, but foodies prefer theirs organic and with flashes of culinary brilliance – and Alaska delivers. Taste buds applaud the roasted-pistachio gelato, but are confounded by the *carciofi*. Could that savoury, barely sweet cream with a subtle minty flavour really be *artichoke*? Yes – and it's stunning paired with the tangy lemon. The celery-peach combo may strike you as a smoothie gone wrong but, at just €1.60 for a double cone, you can afford to take culinary risks.

☞ COOP *Self-Catering*
☎ 041 2960621; Piazzale Roma; ☿ 9am-1pm & 4-7.30pm Mon-Sat; ⚓ Piazzale Roma
Find yourself a *campo* or canalside spot and enjoy an exceptional picnic with supplies from Coop, a supermarket that has prime takeaway, basics and biscuits, all under enticing spotlighting. The branch at Piazzale Rome is the biggest supermarket in the city centre, and its olive and meat selections are

sublime. There's another branch at Campo San Giacomo dell'Orio.

🍴 GELATERIA SAN STAE
Gelato €

☎ 041 710689; Salizada di San Stae 1910; ⏰ 11am-9pm Tue-Sun; 🚊 San Stae

Simple flavours are anything but at San Stae, where the signature ingredients – ranging from Piedmont hazelnut to Madagascar vanilla – are gathered from near and far. Happiness is at hand with a €1 vanilla cone, but heaven is the €2 double with local pistachio.

🍴 IL REFOLO
Inventive Venetian, Pizza €€

☎ 041 5240016; Campo San Giacomo dell'Orio 1459; ⏰ 7pm-midnight Tue, 11am-4pm & 7pm-midnight Wed-Sun; 🚊 Riva di Biasio

Come to Il Refolo for unlikely pizzas and unexpectedly chic style on a quiet *campo*. Prices are higher than you might expect, but on sunny days and starlit nights a meal in the *campo* with a glass of wine from the well-curated cellar is ideal. Pizza is only served from April to October and toppings are seasonal, but if your timing is right you might luck onto the pizza with zucchini flowers and crescenza cheese, or the one with *lardo* (cured pork fat) and *castraure* (baby artichokes).

🍴 MURO ꜰ
☎ 041 52416ꜱ
.com; Campiello ꜱ
⏰ noon-11pm; ꜱ

Mellow at lunch hour and chic at ꜱ, this versatile restaurant-bar-pizzeria aims to please. Grab a chair in the piazza, or duck into the snug exposed-brick interior for prime seating on white-leather-and-striped-silk banquettes. Inventive pizza makes a reasonable-but-not-overly-cheap date, lighting is shamelessly flattering, and the beer and wine selection is above average – sounds like a recipe for romance, no?

🍴 OSTERIA AE CRAVATE
Classic Venetian €€

☎ 041 5287912; Salizada San Pantalon 36; ⏰ 9.30am-4pm & 6-11pm Tue-Sun; 🚊 Riva de Biasio

A mosquito-motif tie loosened by a ravenous British entomologist is Bruno's favourite of the trophy ties hanging from the ceiling, all donated by grateful diners who would risk their necks (or at least their neckties) for his fresh pasta. Don't get cheeky and demand bow-tie pasta; instead, choose rustic ravioli with sage and brown butter, or slender tagliolitti with shrimp and zucchini flowers. Leave room for the home-baked desserts.

Spice up your life with a meal at Osteria La Zucca

🍴 OSTERIA LA ZUCCA
Mediterranean　　　　€€
☎ 041 5241570; www.lazucca.it; Calle del Tentor 1762; 🕑 12.30-2.30pm & 7-10.30pm Mon-Sat; 🚢 San Stae

When plates of pasta seem too much and *cicheti* (Venetian tapas) too little, La Zucca is just right. Vegetablecentric Mediterranean small plates (€5 to €8) bring spice-trade influences to bear on local produce: zucchini comes with a ginger zing, carrots get curried with yoghurt, and rice pudding goes down easily with strawberries. Vegetarians can placate carnivorous travelling companions with roast lamb options, but veggies have the star quality here.

🍴 VECIO FRITOLIN
Inventive Venetian,
Sustainable Eating　　　€€€
☎ 041 5222881; www.veciofritolin.it; Calle della Regina 2262; 🕑 noon-2.30pm & 7-10.30pm Tue-Sun; 🚢 San Stae

Peer past all the Slow Food awards plastered on the windows, and you'll spot a sign of the delicious food to come: blissed-out Italian foodies footing substantial lunch bills without flinching. Recent standouts include tender spider crab atop tagliolini made from beetroot, all served in the crab shell; a heart-warming nettle soup; and oven-baked lamb chops with sweet onions and roast potatoes. But since all the produce is hand

picked daily at the Rialto markets –
it's never canned or frozen –
trust your savvy server to know
what's best today. Gourmets on
the go call ahead for the €10 fried-
fish takeaway.

🍸 DRINK

🍸 AL PROSECCO *Wine Bar*

☎ 041 5240222; Campo San Giacomo
dell'Orio 1503; ⏱ 8am-10pm; 🚢 Riva
di Biasio

Head to this bar for delightful
prosecco without the pretence in
a hidden gem of a *campo*. Sample
a range of prosecco and other
Veneto wines by the glass under
a sun umbrella or with the locals
at the bar, then when the bubbles ascend and protein seems
advisable, order a platter of mixed
cured meats or local cheeses.
They're large enough to share, and
this is the kind of congenial place
where you might invite others to
help you finish without it seeming
the least bit odd.

🍸 LA RIVETTA *Pub*

Calle Sechera 637a; ⏱ 9am-9.30pm
Mon-Sat; 🚢 Ferrovia

Cabernet franc comes out of a
hose and platters of hearty fare

are passed around at this favourite
bacaro (bar) of salty sailors and
neighbourhood eccentrics. Go
for mixed plates with thick slabs
of salami, translucent sheets of
pancetta and grilled veggies with
crusty bread. You can sit canalside,
or head inside to admire the decor
of bicycle parts and dusty bottles
of English gin that were drained
before the war. Buy a round to
bring down the house.

⭐ PLAY

⭐ AI POSTALI *Live Music*

☎ 041 715156; Fondamenta Rio Marin
421; ⏱ 6pm-2am Mon-Sat; 🚢 Rivo di
Biasio

You won't find the live music
here on any event calendar – it's
completely spontaneous. Jazz
usually plays on the stereo until
10pm or so, when local musicians
converge on the marble bar for
spritz (prosecco-based cocktail)
served with an olive. By last call,
jam sessions have often erupted.
This is about the only place in Venice that gets away with a cityscape
fresco without seeming touristy,
simply because the home-town
pride here isn't for show, it's the
real deal.

>DORSODURO

In other cities, arty neighbourhoods are gritty, marginal districts that are best appreciated by grunge bands and collage artists. But Dorsoduro claims the very heart of the city and, instead of gloomy backstreet galleries, it has palatial buildings along the Grand Canal: Ca' Rezzonico, the Peggy Guggenheim Collection and the Gallerie dell'Accademia. There's far more glam than grit here, even in unlikely places. Paolo Veronese lavished his tiny neighbourhood church with masterpieces; Giambattista Tiepolo and Baldassare Longhena worked wonders on a convent that doubled as a hostel; and minimalist maestro Tadao Ando is set to complete the Punta della Dogana's transformation from warehouse dock to contemporary-art showcase. But, somehow, this lavish attention hasn't gone to Dorsoduro's head. The neighbourhood still convenes nightly in Campo Santa Margherita for happy hour, queues up along the Zattere for gelato on sunny days, and haggles over the price of tomatoes at the produce barge alongside Campo San Barnaba.

DORSODURO

Please see over for map

◉ SEE

◉ CA' REZZONICO

☎ 041 2410100; www.museiciviciven eziani.it; Fondamenta Rezzonico 3136; adult/EU 6-14yr, student & over 65yr €6.50/4.50; ⏱ 10am-6pm Wed-Mon Apr-Oct, 10am-5pm Wed-Mon Nov-Mar, ticket office closes 1hr earlier; 🚊 Ca' Rezzonico

Other museums may illuminate, but this one sparkles. This Longhena palace showcases 18th-century arts in music salons, boudoirs and even a pharmacy complete with medicinal scorpions. Several salons are crowned with ceilings by Tiepolo, who literally goes over the top with his sensuous beauty and shameless flattery. His Throne Room ceiling is a glimpse of heaven at the moment gorgeous Merit ascends to the Temple of Glory, clutching the Libro d'Oro (Golden Book), which contained the names of Venetian nobles – including the Rezzonico family, naturally. Other collection highlights include Pietro Longhi's socialite satires, Guercino's dashing *Philosopher* and Emma Ciardi's pointillist canal views. Don't miss concerts by Venice's Chamber Music Orchestra held in the ballroom. See p22 for more.

◉ CHIESA DEI GESUATI

☎ 041 5230625; Zattere 918; adult/under 5yr €3/free, with Chorus pass free; ⏱ 10am-5pm Mon-Sat; 🚊 Zattere

If you're not yet sold on baroque art, just look up. On ceiling panels completed between 1737 and 1739, Tiepolo uses convincing architectural perspectives and heavenly colours that seem to lift the roof right off the place to tell stories from the life of St Dominic. On the right side of the nave is the 1730–33 *Saints Peter and Thomas with Pope Pius V* by fellow Venetian virtuoso of luminosity Sebastiano Ricci; it's quite a contrast to Tintoretto's adjacent 1565 *Crucifixion*, which glowers darkly in deep reds and greens. In this church, Venetian baroque puts the city's dark plague days in the past, ushering the sunny Zattere indoors instead.

◉ CHIESA DI SAN SEBASTIAN

☎ 041 5282487; Campo San Sebastian; admission €3, with Chorus pass free; ⏱ 10am-5pm Mon-Sat; 🚊 San Basilio

Only in Venice could a modest neighbourhood church be covered with floor-to-ceiling Veronese masterpieces. Veronese's horses rear over the frames of the coffered ceiling, his angels literally come out of the woodwork and even the organ doors are covered inside and out with vivid Veronese works. The only thing more colourful than his brushwork is the popular legend that claims Veronese found sanctuary here in 1555 when he fled murder accusations in Verona; as

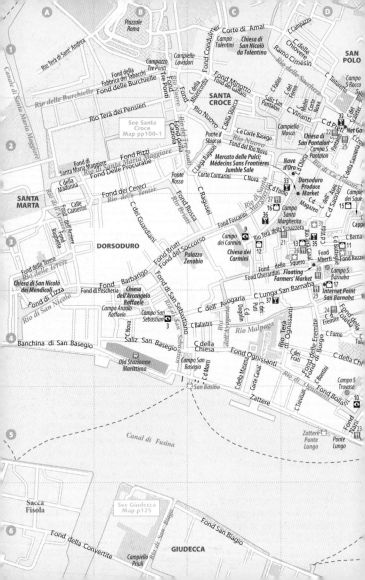

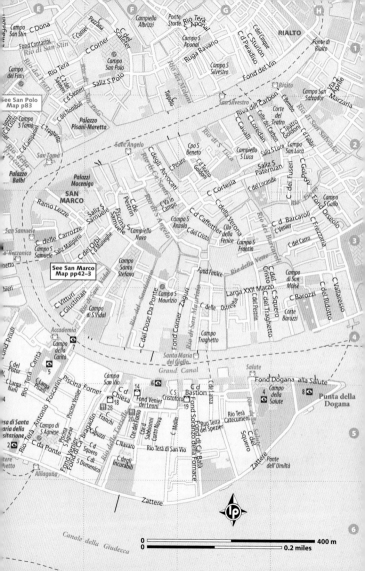

SESTIERI

DORSODURO

Angels in the architecture: gaze at Veronese's heavenly pictures in the Chiesa di San Sebastian (p109)

a result, he couldn't do enough to thank the parish. This story casts a different light on Veronese's *Martyrdom of St Sebastian,* where the bound saint defiantly stares down his tormentors amid a local crowd of fashionable nobles, turbaned traders and, for comic relief, a frisky lapdog.

⊙ CHIESA DI SANTA MARIA DELLA SALUTE

☎ 041 5225558; Campo della Salute; church free, sacristy €1.50; ☽ 9am–noon & 5-5.30pm; 🚊 Salute

Survivors of Venice's 1630 plague built Our Lady of Salvation atop at least 100,000 pylons as a monumental gesture of thanks,

and Venetians still pray for health here at least once a year (p30). Architectural scholars have noticed the similarity between Longhena's unusual octagonal design, and both Graeco-Roman temples and Jewish cabbala diagrams; after the horrors of the plague, covering multiple religious traditions must've seemed like a wise health-insurance policy. The sacristy here holds Tintoretto's surprisingly upbeat *Wedding Feast of Cana,* plus no fewer than 12 Titians (see p16), including *St Marco Enthroned* (his earliest known work, from 1510) and a later *St Matthew* that's actually a self-portrait.

GALLERIE DELL'ACCADEMIA

☎ 041 5222247; www.gallerieacc
ademia.org; Campo della Carità 1050;
adult/EU 6-14yr, student & over 65yr
€6.50/3.25; ⏱ 8.15am-2pm Mon,
8.15am-7.15pm Tue-Sun, ticket office
closes 45min earlier; 👤 Accademia

A multiplicity of masterpieces await
behind the serene walls of this
former convent. All the superstars
of Venetian art are well represented
here: Titian's red-hot sensuality,
Tintoretto's action-packed drama,
Vittore Carpaccio's gore-fests, Giovanni Bellini's Holy Family bonding
moments, Rosalba Carriera's un-
Botoxed portraits, and Veronese's
censored social commentary.
Galleries are loosely organised
by painter and time period; you'll
have to pace yourself so you're not
tempted to rush past Rooms 16 to
18, which are packed with remarkable portraits, Canaletto's sweeping
views of Venice, and Giorgione's
1508 *La Tempesta,* an expressionist
composition of blues and greens
that was centuries ahead of its time.

PEGGY GUGGENHEIM COLLECTION

☎ 041 2405411; www.guggenheim
-venice.it; Palazzo Venier dei Leoni,
Fondamenta Venier dei Leone 701; adult/
student under 26yr/senior/under 10yr
€10/5/8/free; ⏱ 10am-6pm Wed-Mon;
👤 Accademia

The possessor o[...]
she lost her fath[...]
Peggy Guggenh[...]
dadaists and dod[...]
amassing avant-g[...] works
by 200 modern artists. Peggy's
palatial home is a now a modernist shrine highlighting Italian
futurism, surrealist painting, and
key works by ground-breaking
expressionists Wassily Kandinsky,
her ex-husband Max Ernst and
Jackson Pollock (one of Peggy's
many rumoured lovers). Since
Peggy didn't collect for prestige,
her art collection also features
wonderful folk art and lesser-
known artists, plus comparatively
minor works by Pablo Picasso,
Piet Mondrian and Salvador Dalí.
Rather than following a favourite
medium or trend, Peggy collected
according to her own modernist
ideals, and her sensibilities can
be glimpsed throughout these
galleries.

PONTE DELL'ACCADEMIA

👤 Accademia

The steep wooden hump over the
Grand Canal has put Accademia-
bound tourists through their pac-
es since 1930. The timber structure
was meant to be a temporary
replacement for a 19th century
metal bridge, but the craftsman-
ship was too sturdy and the views
from the top far too thrilling to
even think of scrapping it.

TREASURE HUNTS

You might not be able to find St Mark's missing kneecap inside the Basilica di San Marco or the Bellini that was whisked off the walls at Madonna dell'Orto in 1993, but other treasures await discovery in Venice.

Sunny summer weekends bring the *mercato delle pulci* (flea market) to the Campo Santa Margherita, along with the occasional Médecins Sans Frontières jumble sale, organised by two charming Venetian brothers who decided that retirement is boring, and the world needs all the help it can get. At these markets you'll spot antique Murano stemware, tiny copper pots in which you could cook *cicheti* (Venetian tapas) for dolls, and vintage Italian fashion magazines that have been hoarded in Venetian attics for decades.

Bochaleri in Campo (Map pp42–3, C5; www.bochaleri.it; Campo San Maurizio, San Marco; ☯ 9am-5pm last weekend of May; ☖ Santa Maria del Giglio), the annual ceramics market, covers styles and eras ranging from classic Renaissance portrait plates to the latest *raku* (a style of Japanese pottery) pieces.

The **Mercantino dei Miracoli** (☯ 9am-1pm & 3.30-7.30pm 1st weekend every month; ☖ Ca' d'Oro), which takes place either in Campo Santa Maria Nova (Map pp72–3, G6) or Via Garibaldi, and **Mercantino dell'Antiquario** (Map pp42–3, C5; ☎ 333 9659994; www .mercantinosanmaurizio.it; Campo San Maurizio; ☯ 9am-5pm last weekend of every month; ☖ Santa Maria del Giglio) sell antique ceramics, estate jewellery, tempestuous seascapes, Fellini-esque vintage sunglasses and bric-a-brac at prices that approach those of Sotheby's. Still, the scene is more raucously colourful than you'll find at auction houses and, honestly, where else are you going to buy a gondola prow?

◉ PUNTA DELLA DOGANA
☖ Salute

Finally Venice can release the breath it's been holding since François Pinault announced that Tadao Ando would be transforming this block of warehouses into Venice's newest monument to contemporary art. Barring some twist of Fortune – the weather vane atop Punta Dogana, that is – Pinault's art collection will be installed in 2009 in a modernised structure that preserves the character of the original customs houses.

◉ SCUOLA GRANDE DEI CARMINI

☎ 041 5289420; Campo Santa Margherita 2617; adult/student/child €5/4/2; ☯ 9am-5pm Mon-Sat, 9am-4pm Sun Apr-Oct, 9am-4pm Nov-Mar; ☖ Ca' Rezzonico

Eighteenth-century backpackers must have thought they'd died and gone to heaven at the Scuola Grande dei Carmini – up the most gorgeous staircase in Venice, to the right past Tiepolo's nine-panel ceiling of a resplendent *Virgin in Glory*, and through heavy doors was the lavish boiserie (carved timber) hostel where Carmelite nuns sheltered wayfarers. Cots are, sadly, no longer available in this jewel-box building, but the **Venice Opera** (www.venice-opera.com) sometimes stages performances here.

🇨 SQUERO DI SAN TROVASO
Campo San Trovaso 1097; 🚉 Zattere
When it's time for a tune up, gondolieri head to the *squero* (gondola workshop). The wood cabin on the corner of the Rio di San Trovaso may look like a misplaced ski chalet, but it's actually part of one of the city's three working *squeri*. From the right bank, you can see refinished gondolas drying in the yard, and wave at Cristina della Toffola (p143) in her *bragosso* (Venetian barge).

🛍 SHOP
🇨 ANTICHITÀ TERESA BALLARIN *Antiques*
☎ 041 2771807; Calle delle Botteghe 3184; 🕙 4-7pm Mon, 10am-1pm & 3-7pm Tue-Sat; 🚉 Ca' Rezzonico
Fabulous finds in styles ranging from rococo to rock and roll prove Venice's fashion heyday didn't end with baroque. Antique vases and paintings make fitting souvenirs, but 20th-century pieces are the real scores: futurist Bakelite rings, the odd Scarpa lamp, a rare ceramic vase by Gio Ponti and an op-art ladybird brooch, all for about what

you'd pay for derivative works by modern designers.

🇨 AQUA ALTRA
Gifts, Sustainable Shopping
☎ 041 5211259; www.aquaaltra.it; Campo Santa Margherita 2898; 🕙 4-7.30pm Mon, 9.30am-12.30pm & 4-7.30pm Tue-Sat; 🚉 Ca' Rezzonico
Venice has learned a thing or two about trading nicely with others since the days when it controlled maritime trade – hence this fair-trade boutique. Italian taste is matched with global conscience in single-origin chocolate from Sierra Leone cooperatives, footballs made by a Pakistani cooperative, and stuffed African-fabric alligators that support artisans in Kenya.

🇨 GUALTI *Jewellery*
☎ 041 5201731; www.gualti.it; Rio Terà Canal 3111; 🕙 10am-1pm & 3-7.30pm Mon-Sat; 🚉 Ca' Rezzonico
Either a shooting star just landed on your shoulder, or you've been to Gualti. Iridescent orange glass bursts from clear resin stems on an interstellar brooch, while metallic pink fused Lucite cascades from an invisible collar like fireworks. Like light displays on the lagoon, these movable pieces stir the imagination. Gualti doesn't like to repeat himself, but his prices (starting at €70) are less than you'd expect for one-off designs.

Marina Sent
Architect turned pioneering glass designer at
Marina e Susanna Sent (opposite)

Shattering the glass ceiling My family have been glass designers in Murano for generations. But back in the '80s, glass-blowing was a profession dominated by men, and my background was in architecture. So when my sister and I began working in glass, it was just for fun, to see what we could do. Glass jewellery wasn't part of the family tradition, and we wanted to make something new. **Spicing it up** Anyone interested in glass should visit the Museo del Vetro [p142], and explore Murano to look inside laboratories and hear the furnaces. But design inspiration is everywhere in Venice: lately I've been inspired by spices, the piles of paprika and cinnamon at the Rialto markets [p94]. **Angels in the architecture** As medieval artisans paid for the capitals along the Ducal Palace [p45], we financed the restoration of the statue of Virtue on the side of the building – it's our honour to continue the artisans' tradition in the heart of Venice.

IL PAVONE *Paper Crafts*

☎ 041 5234517; Calle della Chiesa 721; ⏰ 10am-1pm & 3-6pm Tue-Sat; 🚇 Accademia

Your *baccalà mantecato* (mashed cod prepared in garlic and parsley) is bound to come out better when the recipe is captured in a handmade book stamped with Gothic architectural patterns. Il Pavone's recipe books, travel journals and day planners are printed with traces of metallic pigments, but don't just judge them by their shimmering covers. Inside, the books are well organised, with tabs for meal planning, headings to track your favourite sights and spots to note upcoming birthdays.

L'ANGOLO DEL PASSATO *Antiques*

☎ 041 5287896; Campiello dei Squellini 3276; ⏰ 10am-1pm & 3-6pm Tue-Sat; 🚇 Ca' Rezzonico

Turn left off baroque, head straight into modern, and you'll end up at this corner antique shop. Displays are frighteningly fragile, ranging from time-tarnished baroque mirrors with inset candelabra to mod swirled-colour water glasses. The best finds are oddities from the 1920s to 1970s, including dramatic deco pitchers, and smoked-glass lamps that set a bachelor-pad mood.

LIBRERIA DEL CAMPO *Books*

☎ 041 5210624; Campo Santa Margherita 2943; ⏰ 10am-10pm Mon-Sat; 🚇 Ca' Rezzonico

Discounted books and unusual coffee-table tomes make this a perennial favourite with the student crowd. There are some English-language titles from international publishers such as Taschen, plus splashy Italian art books from the likes of Rizzoli.

MADERA *Gifts, Homewares*

☎ 041 5224181; www.maderavenezia.it; Campo San Barnaba 2762; ⏰ 10am-1pm & 3-6pm Tue-Sat; 🚇 Ca' Rezzonico

Frying pans look like clocks, spoons become tongues, and wooden salad bowls curl into waves: at Madera, household objects are transformed by elemental materials and organic shapes. Most pieces are by owner-designer Francesca Meratti and other Italian designers, with some Scandinavian and Japanese influences; prices start below €70 for steel-and-pearl rings and free-form wooden spoons.

MARINA E SUSANNA SENT *Glass, Jewellery*

☎ 041 5208136; www.marinaesusannasent.com; Campo San Vio 669; ⏰ 10am-1pm & 3-6.30pm Tue-Sat, 3-6.30pm Mon; 🚇 Accademia

Megaphones are no longer necessary to stand out in a

SESTIERI

DORSODURO

crowd, thanks to this whip-smart statement jewellery by pioneering glass designers Marina and Susanna Sent (see p116). Museum shops throughout Venice feature the sisters' signature 'soap' necklaces: large, clear bubbles of thin yet surprisingly sturdy glass that bring a sense of humour to boardrooms and first dates. Glass is paired with unexpected materials in dramatic red-paper necklaces with oversized red-glass centrepieces, while an asymmetrical black leather collar is decorated with dollops of glass that look like teaspoons of paprika and saffron.

PASTOR *Woodcarving*
☎ 041 5225699; www.forcole.com; Fondamenta Soranzo della Fornace 341; 8.30am-12.30pm & 2.30-6pm Mon-Sat; 🛥 Salute

The *forcola* (forked tongue of wood where the gondola oar rests) for a gondola is hand carved from acacia and hard oak, and each *forcola* must hold up under pressure and express the style of its owner. Sounds like a job for Saverio Pastor, who makes *forcole* that twist without losing their elegant balance – just like the most experienced gondolieri. Mick Jagger had his *forcola* made to measure here, but you can buy ready-made smaller *forcole* to display as sculpture.

Blooming marvellous: Dorsoduro's flower stalls

EAT

AI GONDOLIERI
Inventive Venetian €€€
☎ 041 5286396; www.aigondolieri.com; Fondamenta Ospedaleto 366; noon-3pm & 7-10pm Wed-Mon; 🛥 Accademia

The front window may be facing the canal, but the menu here is strictly landlocked. Carnivores on a seafood strike can tuck into ravioli stuffed with pheasant and lamb, but there are also some decadent dishes for vegetarians, including the cheesy polenta torte with a rich leek-bean sauce. Order the silky marzipan-laced tiramisu before fellow diners such as Meryl Streep or Woody Allen snap up the last one.

🍴 AI SPORTIVI *Pizza* €

☎ 041 5211598; Campo Santa Margherita 3052; 🕐 noon-10pm Mon-Sat; 🚇 Ca' Rezzonico

When you need something to eat even *before* you get to the Ca' Rezzonico, head to Ai Sportivi – stat! Within minutes, thin-crust pizzas topped with gorgonzola, ham or seasonal vegetables are served to you by speedy, cheerful waiters.

🍴 ANTICA PASTICCERIA TONOLO *Pastries* €

☎ 041 5327209; Calle dei Preti 3764; 🕐 8am-8pm Mon-Sat, 8am-1pm Sun; 🚇 Ca' Rezzonico

Dire B&B breakfasts with packaged croissants are corrected at Tonolo, which serves flaky apple strudel and oozing *pain au chocolat* (chocolate croissants). Tide yourself through an early-evening concert with espresso and chocolate-topped beignets, their hazelnut-mousse filling as rich as a Venetian doge at tax-time.

🍴 DA NICO *Gelato* €

☎ 041 5225293; Zattere 922; 🕐 7am-10pm Fri-Wed; 🚇 Zattere

Those sunny days when you're feeling too lazy for a trip to the Lido are perfect for Da Nico's dock. Pounce on free seats and order one of the house specialities: the *gianduiotto* (a slab of hazelnut gelato submerged under whipped cream) or *panna in ghiaccio* (frozen whipped cream sandwiched between cookies). Those specialities are half the price if you eat at the bar, but you'll want that seat once the gelato coma sets in.

🍴 ENOTECA AI ARTISTI *Italian* €€

☎ 041 5238944; www.enotecaartisti.com; Fondamenta de la Toletta 1169a; 🕐 noon-4pm & 6.30-10pm Mon-Sat; 🚇 Accademia

The heart-warming pastas, seasonal bruschette and inspired cheese selections here can be paired, course by course, with wines by the glass suggested by your oenophile hosts. The glassed-in storefront makes for great people-watching, but space is limited so book ahead for groups larger than two.

🍴 IMPRONTACAFÉ *Italian, Sandwiches* €€

☎ 041 2750386; Calle Crosera 3815; 🕐 11am-11pm Mon-Sat; 🚇 San Tomà

Polenta, prosecco and espresso are the order of the hour, on the hour, for guests who come for lunch and stay through to evening. The best deals here are the mixed-plate combos, especially the grilled polenta with wild mushrooms, Venetian *sopressa* (salami) and salad. Architectural diagrams of cooking pots on blackboards and a Buddha presiding over the bar add a sly sense of humour to the sleek modern decor.

PASTICCERIA GOBBETTI
Pastries   €

☎ 041 5289014; Ponte dei Pugni 3108b;
⏱ 7.30am-8pm; 🚶 Ca' Rezzonico

Why would a chocolate shop need to open so early? As locals know, daybreak is long enough to have to wait for your next dose of Gobetti's chocolate mousse. If you pick up some filled-chocolate doges' caps for the folks back home, you can call your 7.30am trip 'souvenir shopping'.

PIZZA AL VOLO *Pizza*   €

☎ 041 5225430; Campo Santa Margherita 2944; ⏱ noon-1am; 🚶 Ca' Rezzonico

Peckish night owls fast run out of options in Venice after the *cicheti* (Venetian tapas) has gone and the restaurant kitchens have closed – but Pizza Al Volo has you covered. Slices here are cheap and respectable; they don't have a lot of fancy toppings, but they possess a thin yet sturdy crust that won't collapse on your going-out outfit.

RISTORANTE CANTINONE STORICO *Classic Venetian* €€€

☎ 041 5239577; Fondamenta di Ca' Bragadin 660-661; ⏱ noon-3pm & 7-10pm Mon-Sat, closed Nov & Jan;
🚶 Accademia

The canalside seating here is nice, but don't hold out for it – and, once your pasta arrives, it'll command your attention anyway. Tagliatelle with asparagus, prawns and artichokes in *busara* (prawn sauce) may sound simple, but try telling your taste buds. The restaurant's on the expensive side, but it's close to the Gallerie dell'Accademia and serves proper Venetian dishes without cutting corners.

RISTORANTE LA BITTA
Italian   €€€

☎ 041 5230531; Calle Lunga San Barnaba 2753a; ⏱ 7-10pm Mon-Sat;
🚶 Ca' Rezzonico

The daily bill of fare is presented on a miniature artist's easel, which is fair enough: the short, stout seasonal menu is a thing of beauty for anyone craving a nonseafood dinner. The breast of guinea fowl melts into its mascarpone sauce, the gnocchi with pumpkin is as rich as the Rezzonicos, and the beef fillet is juicy enough to make you want to tuck in that napkin. The restaurant doesn't offer wine by the glass, but the staff will cut you a deal on a half bottle.

RISTOTECA ONIGA
Classic Venetian   €€

☎ 041 5224410; www.oniga.it; Campo San Barnaba 2852; ⏱ noon-3pm & 7-10pm Wed-Mon; 🚶 Ca' Rezzonico

CLASS ACTS

Learn the local lingo, whip up a Venetian signature dish, row along Giudecca or go incognito in a self-made mask with the following courses.

Devise your own disguise for Carnevale – or for back at the office when the boss is looking for you – at **Ca' Macana** (☎ 041 5229749; www.camacana.com; Calle delle Botteghe 3172; class about €60; ⏰ 3pm Wed & Fri; 🚉 Ca' Rezzonico). Two-and-a-half-hour courses on mask making and mask decorating are held in English in this backstreet artisanal mask-making studio; the bigger the group, the less it costs per head.

Get to know Venice from the inside out with English-language courses run by the **Friends of Venice Club** (☎ 041 715877; www.friendsofveniceclub.com; 🚉 Ca' Rezzonico). Classes include Italian cookery; chamber-music and choral performances in a local *palazzo* (palace or mansion); Venetian rowing; and plein-air drawing and painting all around town. Instructors are patient and genuinely enthusiastic about showing you the Venice they love.

At **Istituto Venezia** (☎ 041 5224331; www.istitutovenezia.com; Campo Santa Margherita 3116a; course per week €160-540; 🚉 Ca' Rezzonico) you can learn Italian by day in Campo Santa Margherita, then join the happy-hour small talk afterwards. Language classes or combined language-and-art courses run for one week or longer, and cater for all levels of experience. If you want to be the star pupil, consider one-on-one tutoring, which is charged by the hour. Prices for courses vary according to class size, intensiveness and duration.

Purists come for chef Annika's *nervetti* (calf's tendons) and Venetian liver with onions, while gourmet rebels order the springtime-in-your-mouth ravioli with ricotta, broccoli and poppy seeds off the quirky seasonal menu. Either way you can't lose, and piazza seating and smooth service only sweeten the deal.

🍴 TRATTORIA DONA ONESTA
Classic Venetian €

☎ 041 710586; www.donaonesta.com; Calle Dona Onesta 3922; ⏰ noon-3.30pm & 6.30-10pm; 🚉 San Tomà
At the Honest Woman tavern, devoted regulars are moved to truth

over generous pours of house wine, moaning about Berlusconi, and raving about the vast bowls of mussels and clams: 'The owner's Egyptian, but he cooks like a Venetian.' Vegetarians will enjoy the veggie pasta with a roasted red-capsicum kick, and anyone pinched by euro exchange rates will appreciate the modest bill.

🍸 DRINK
🍸 CAFÉ NOIR *Cafe-Bar*

☎ 041 710925; Calle Crosera 3805; ⏰ 7am-2am Mon-Fri, 5pm-2am Sat, 9am-2am Sun; 🚉 San Tomà
Morning espresso brings back the crowd that was here late last

Bottoms up! Practise your balancing skills at Cantinone 'Gia Schiavi'

night, only a little the worse for wear. Architecture students, musicians and travellers converge for *spritz* (prosecco-based cocktails) in the *calle* (street), so the quickest way to start a conversation is to state any of the following: Calatrava is overrated, Albinoni is underrated, and *spritz* with Aperol is better than *spritz* with Campari.

CAFFÈ ROSSO *Cafe-Bar*
☎ 041 5287998; Campo Santa Margherita 2963; 🕙 7am-1am Mon-Sat; 🚤 Ca' Rezzonico

The red heart of Campo Santa Margherita is this cafe, affectionately nicknamed Rosso after its red front window. Sunny mornings

are well spent at a piazza table, commiserating over newspaper headlines with your neighbours then laughing it off with a prosecco at lunch. Evening brings the student crowd for a *spritz*, with entertainment provided by the cast of characters at the bar.

CANTINONE 'GIA SCHIAVI'
Pub, Wine Bar
☎ 041 5230034; Fondamenta Nani 992; 🕙 8.30am-8.30pm Mon-Sat; 🚤 Accademia

Good lungs and steady hands are essential to make your order heard over Cantinone's happy hour, and to transport your glass of wine or *pallottoline* (small bottle of beer) outside to the canal without spilling it. Students, gondola builders and Accademia art historians all perch on canal railings and along the bridge, but remember: they've had more practice at not falling in than you.

▮ IMAGINA CAFÉ *Cafe-Bar*
☎ 041 2410625; www.imaginacafe.it; Rio Terà Canal 3126; 🕙 9am-2am Tue-Sun; 🚇 Ca' Rezzonico

Comfortable booths, works by emerging artists on the walls and a vast display of Aperol behind the bar all bring a creative, gay-friendly crowd that should probably start paying rent here. Sunny piazza seating is usually thronged with locals and their little dogs, both of whom enjoy being admired.

▮ OSTERIA ALLA BIFORA
Wine Bar
☎ 041 5236119; Campo Santa Margherita 2930; 🕙 10am-2am; 🚇 Ca' Rezzonico

The staff aren't exactly quick with that Ferrari red meat slicer behind the bar, so just sip that wine, soak in the ambience of this romantic Romanesque bar, and don't count on your snacks to arrive any time soon. This place has a more mellow, enticing vibe than

other places on the square, and strangers have been known to get cosy at the communal tables.

▮ TEA ROOM BEATRICE
Tea House
☎ 041 7241042; Calle Lunga San Barnaba 2727a; 🕙 10am-6pm; 🚇 Ca' Rezzonico

This tea house is an elegant alternative to bolting an espresso at a bar. Rainy days are good for iron pots of green tea and almond cake in the Japanese-themed tea room, while sunny days are for iced drinks and salty pistachios on the patio.

PLAY

☆ VENICE JAZZ CLUB *Jazz*
☎ 041 5232056; www.venicejazzclub.com; Ponte dei Pugni 3102; admission incl drink €15; 🕙 from 5.30pm Mon, Wed, Fri & Sat; 🚇 Ca' Rezzonico

This place is suspiciously well-organized for a jazz club, but the Venice Jazz Club Quartet keeps the vibe loose with improvisational tributes to jazz greats such as Miles Davis and Chet Baker. Drinks here are steep, so most locals start on the good stuff with the drink that comes free with admission, then backslide from there. Music starts at 9pm.

SESTIERI

DORSODURO

V

>GIUDECCA

Architecture binges have brought visitors to this corner of the lagoon for centuries, and no wonder – have you seen the Palladios? But this garden getaway for Venice's elite became the city's industrial outpost in the 19th century, resulting in an industrial sprawl of factories and apartment blocks. Giudecca earns street cred for being affordable and rough around the edges – and, like most city neighbourhoods that used to be industrial and iffy, it has recently become extremely cool. Defunct factories and waterfront warehouses have been converted to galleries, affordable lofts and a theatre, and although there's still a women's prison here, it's near a new luxe spa and a Harry's Bar offshoot. So, hop on the vaporetto (city ferry) to Giudecca now, while the air is electric with creative possibility and prices are still artist-friendly.

GIUDECCA

◉ SEE
Chiesa di San Giorgio
   Maggiore......................1 F1
Fondazione Giorgio
   Cini 2 F2
Giudecca 795.................3 A2
Il Redentore...................4 D3

🛍 SHOP
Fortuny Tessuti
   Artistici.......................5 A2

🍽 EAT
Ai Tre Scalini...................6 E2

Al Pontil dea Giudecca ...7 D3
Harry's Dolci 8 B2
I Figli delle Stelle............9 E2

⭐ PLAY
Casanova Spa 10 E2
Teatro Junghans...........11 B3

👁 SEE

👁 CHIESA DI SAN GIORGIO MAGGIORE

☎ 041 5227827; Isola di San Giorgio Maggiore; church free, bell tower €3; 🕑 9.30am-12.30pm & 2.30-6.30pm Mon-Sat May-Sep, 9.30am-12.30pm & 2.30-4.30pm Mon-Sat Oct-Apr; 🚢 San Giorgio

Sunglasses become essential as you approach San Giorgio – this Andrea Palladio–designed masterpiece is set to dazzle. The white Istrian marble facade is almost blinding head-on, but close up you'll notice the depth of the massive columns that support the tympanum, with the echoing triangles representing the Holy Trinity. This is possibly the only Venetian church where, once inside, you'll have to remind yourself to look at the paintings. Ceilings billow above, and high windows fill the space with filtered sunshine and easy grace. The black, white and red inlaid-stone floor will draw you toward the altar, which is flanked by two Tintoretto masterpieces: *Collecting the Manna* and *The Last Supper*. Sebastiano Ricci's sweet *Madonna Enthroned with Child and Saints* evokes an audible 'aww', as does the stirring panorama from atop the bell tower.

Grab those shades: Palladio's Chiesa di San Giorgio Maggiore is simply dazzling

PALLADIO: LOOKING GOOD AT 500

Before virtually every pillared bank and cupola-capped manor in the British Empire modelled itself on his designs, Andrea Palladio (1508--80) created churches and villas of surpassing lightness and strength in his native Veneto. Palladian facades across the Veneto were scrubbed until gleaming for the 500th anniversary of his birth in 2008, so now is the prime time to see his signature white marble edifices in all their near-blinding glory.

While romantics may be content to contemplate the gleaming facades of **Chiesa di San Giorgio Maggiore** (opposite) or **Il Redentore** (p128) from across the canal, architecture aficionados will want to get up close to appreciate the play of light and shade in multifaceted buildings, and step inside to see how vaulting, roof trusses and high windows create billowing, cloudlike ceilings. Once you're inside the buildings, John Ruskin's sniffy 19th-century denunciations of Palladio as a wannabe Roman architect seem hard to fathom. In these generous halls, the soaring uplift of Gothic architecture and the rational geometry of the Renaissance mingle seamlessly. Note the scrolled-paper capitals and the spare, clean surfaces; in them, you'll see precocious hints of rococo and even the historically minded high modernism of Le Corbusier and Tadao Ando.

● FONDAZIONE GIORGIO CINI

☎ 041 2710280; www.cini.it; Isola di San Giorgio Maggiore; ⊗ exhibitions 10am-6.30pm Mon-Sat; ⛴ San Giorgio

Before American heiresses and French billionaires got involved, culture in Venice was quietly being saved by Vittorio Cini. After escaping the Dachau concentration camp with his son Giorgio, he returned to Venice on a mission to save the Isola di San Giorgio Maggiore, which in 1949 was a ramshackle mess. His foundation bought and converted the island into a centre for arts and maritime culture, and recently converted a defunct nautical academy into a shipshape gallery space. Recent exhibition highlights include a

Giuseppe Santomaso retrospective, which included *Letters to Palladio,* a series of abstract paintings of envelopes with Palladian proportions.

● GIUDECCA 795

☎ 340 8798327; www.giudecca795 .com; Fondamenta San Biagio 795; ⊗ exhibitions 3.30-8pm Tue-Fri, 11am-8pm Sat & Sun; ⛴ Palanca

Do you follow the Titian colourists or do you go with the Tintoretto flow? Either way, Giudecca 795 has you in mind. It features contemporary artists with a strong sense of colour and dynamic line; look for Vito Campanelli's high-impact all-red paintings and Guitamachi's graphic train-track cityscapes.

IL REDENTORE
☎ 041 5231415; Campo del Redentore 194; admission €3, with Chorus pass free; ⏱ 10am-5pm Mon-Sat, 1-5pm Sun; 🛥 Redentore

The Black Death inspired this buoyant white church – started by Palladio in 1577 and finished by Antonio da Ponte in 1592 – which was commissioned in gratitude for the city's survival. There are some appealingly garish paintings by Gerolamo Bassano that look like black velvet, and a characteristically stormy *Ascension* by Tintoretto and his school, but the most memorable work here is often overlooked: Paolo Piazza's 1619 *Gratitude of Venice for Liberation from the Plague*. Piazza shows the city held aloft by angels, using sombre grey tones and simple outlines to capture plague survivors' gratitude and guilt in a way that's strikingly modern.

🛍 SHOP

FORTUNY TESSUTI ARTISTICI *Homewares, Textiles*
☎ 041 5224078; www.fortuny.com; Fondamenta San Biagio 805; ⏱ 9am-1pm & 2-6pm Mon-Fri, 9-11am & 2-6pm Sat & Sun; 🛥 Redentore

At this design showroom, discover the subtly printed, elegantly draped silken fabrics that caused Marcel Proust to wax nostalgic. Fabrication methods have been jealously guarded for almost 100 years, and have yielded over 260 textile designs.

🍴 EAT

AI TRE SCALINI
Classic Venetian €€
☎ 041 5224790; Calle Michelangelo 53c; ⏱ noon-3pm Mon & Fri, noon-3pm & 7-10pm Tue, Wed, Sat & Sun; 🛥 Zitelle

Ouch. Belly laughs hurt after the generous plates of pasta and seafood here – not that that stops anyone. Families hold court on weekends, friends converge for lunch in the garden, and wine flows straight from the barrel.

Il Redentore: a white church for the Black Death

Davide Amadio
Interpreti Veneziani (p97) cellist with a rock-star following

Fish and art on Giudecca A couple of decades ago, Giudecca was mostly fishermen. Now you can find art shows, theatre, musicians – and still plenty of fish. **How baroque is like punk** Baroque composers experienced all the same emotions we do now – fear, passion, violence – back when people lived short, intense lives. We can play politely, or we can be true to the spirit of their work. **Jamming on a 1787 cello** This instrument was made for Venetian churches, with their perfect humidity and generous acoustics. When we travel, the wood dries and contracts, and I have to adjust how I play to get the right sound. **Soundtrack to Tintoretto** It's a tremendous privilege and challenge to play among Tintoretto's masterpieces at Scuola Grande di San Rocco [p86] – we're surrounded by giants. Because Tintoretto is so captivating, you have to work harder to bring people back to the present moment. But that's always true in Venice, right?

Checking out the sweet view at Harry's Dolci

⚍ AL PONTIL DEA GIUDECCA
Classic Venetian €€

☎ 041 5286985; Calle Redentore 197a;
🕙 noon-3.30pm Mon-Fri; ⚓ Redentore
Asking for a menu here is like asking for one at your grandma's house. You'll have one of the three daily specials and like it – really – and by the time lunch is over you'll feel like you should offer to help tidy up.

⚍ HARRY'S DOLCI
Inventive Venetian, Pastries €€€

☎ 041 5224844; www.cipriani
.com; Fondamenta San Biagio 773;
🕙 10.30am-11pm Wed-Mon Apr-Oct;
⚓ Palanca

The service is low-key and the decor retro at this home away from home for the designer-sunglasses crowd, and though the prices have certainly kept up with inflation – think €15 for coffee and homemade *dolci* (dessert) – you could easily linger long enough to write whole novels. With views of the Zattere, and divine lemon tart served under the waterfront sun canopy, what's the rush?

⚍ I FIGLI DELLE STELLE
Inventive Venetian €€

☎ 041 5230004; www.ifiglidellestelle
.it; Fondamente delle Zitelle 70;
🕙 noon-3.30pm & 7pm-midnight Tue-Sat, noon-2.30pm Sun; ⚓ Zitelle

SESTIERI

GIUDECCA

Declarations of love at Venice's most romantic restaurant are slightly suspect – are you sure that's not the food talking? At I Figli delle Stelle, Luigi combines the velvety textures and heart-warming rustic fare of his native Puglia with the light touch and come-hither produce of Venice. A simple broad-bean cream soup with chicory and fresh tomatoes coats the tongue in a very naughty way, while ordering the mixed grill for two with langoustine, sole and fresh sardines hints that this could be serious (though many mains cost under €10). Book a waterfront table with San Marco views or canoodle on the leather couches inside.

⭐ PLAY

⭐ CASANOVA SPA *Spa*
☎ 041 5207744; Hotel Cipriani 10;
🚹 Zitelle

The notorious hedonist who hid out on Giudecca has inspired some decadent spa services, ranging from baroque hand treatments with rejuvenating Venetian damask rose (€100) to antioxidising gold facials (€150 to €200) where your skin is layered with detoxifying gold leaf.

⭐ TEATRO JUNGHANS
Course, Theatre
☎ 041 720635; www.veneziainscena .com; Piazza Junghans; 🚹 Redentore
Wow Carnevale crowds with your unique costume and convincing portrayal of Venetian nobility, courtesy of Teatro Junghans' workshops on costume design in August, mask-acting in July and September, and commedia dell'arte in August and September. If you'd rather leave that sort of thing to the professionals, check the online calendar for the performance schedule.

LIDO

Even the way it slides off the tongue in Italian sounds luxe and slightly louche: *Leeed*-oh. This 12km barrier island, which once housed the lagoon headquarters and quartered visiting navies, became hot property at the turn of the 20th century as a summer getaway from Venice's dark *calle* (streets) and stinky ebbing canals. Liberty villas and hotels sprung up around the island, the chic set moved in, and overnight the beaches became thronged with cabanas and large-hatted fashionistas. Lately the cabanas have been upgraded to four-poster day beds at beach party spots, and the Lido has increased its star power from solitary supernova Thomas Mann (who set *Death in Venice* here) to red-carpet constellations at the annual Venice Film Festival, held at the Palazzo della Cinema. The cars might come as a shock after a few days in traffic-free Venice, but the best way to get around is still biking – or strutting.

LIDO

◎ SEE
Antico Cimitero
  Israelitico 1 D1
Lido Beaches 2 C4
Palazzo della Cinema 3 B6

🍴 EAT
Da Tiziano 4 A6
Trattoria Andri 5 C4
Trattoria La Favorita 6 D2

🍸 DRINK
Colony Bar 7 C4

⭐ PLAY
Aurora Beach Club 8 D3
Lido on Bike 9 C3
Multisala Astra 10 C3

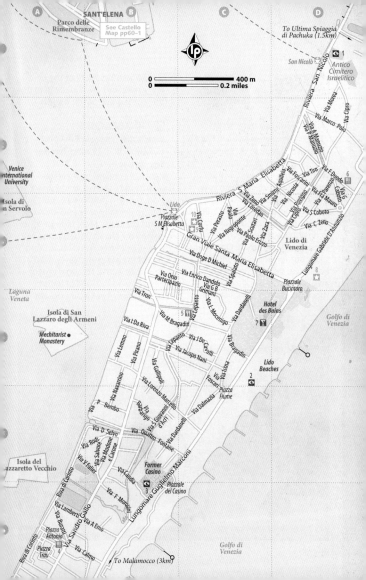

👁 SEE

👁 ANTICO CIMITERO ISRAELITICO

Ancient Jewish Cemetery; ☎ 041 715359; www.museoebraico.it; tour €10; ⏱ tours 3.30pm Sun; 🚤 San Nicolò
Epic poems seem to almost write themselves in this quiet, overgrown garden, which was Venice's main Jewish cemetery from 1386 until the 18th century. As a result, the tombstones range in design from Venetian Gothic to distinctly Ottoman. One-hour tours organised by the Museo Ebraico di Venezia (p75) provide an insight into the life and times of those buried here; English-language tours meet at the cemetery gate and are usually held on the last Sunday of the month.

👁 LIDO BEACHES

deposit/chair/umbrella & chair/hut €5/5.50/11/17; ⏱ 9.30am-7pm May-Sep; 🚤 Lido
Beach chairs and bronzed life-guards may seem a world apart from muggy, ripe Venice, but they're actually only a 15-minute ferry ride away. Most Lido beaches charge for chair, umbrella and hut rental, but after 2pm the tanning crowd thins out and rates drop a couple of euros. To avoid ameni-ties fees and throngs of Italian weekenders, rent a bike and head

Do the Lido shuffle on the island's beaches

BEST. PARTY. EVER

Venice party planners outdid themselves for the reception of young King Henry III of France in 1574. As he approached the city on a royal barge rowed by 400 oarsmen, glass-blowers blew molten glass on rafts alongside the ship for his entertainment. (Sure beats balloon animals!) On arrival, the king was greeted by a bevy of Venetian beauties dressed in white and dripping family jewels into deep décolletages. Then came dinner: 1200 dishes, 300 bonbons and napkins made from spun sugar. But the masterstroke was the all-star decorations committee of Andrea Palladio, Paolo Veronese and Tintoretto, who built and painted triumphal arches for the occasion. Try topping that at your next office party.

south to Alberoni, and other more pristine beaches.

⊙ MALAMOCCO
off Map p133; 🚊 Lido
If Venice got left in the dryer, it might come out as tiny canal-filled Malamocco, the lagoon capital from AD 742 to 811. Pass over Ponte di Borge to explore the *calle* of this less overwhelming lagoon town, which has just a handful of *campi* (squares), churches, *osterie* (restaurant-bars) and grand *palazzi* (palaces or mansions).

⊙ PALAZZO DELLA CINEMA
🚊 Lido
This rigid airport-terminal structure seems as ill-suited to the playboy Lido as a woolly bathing suit. But it all makes sense once the red carpets are rolled out and the stars arrive for the Venice Film Festival (p18): the Palace of Cinema isn't just a party venue, it's a movie-launching platform.

🍴 EAT

🍴 DA TIZIANO *Cicheti, Pizza*
☎ 041 5267291; Via Sandro Gallo 96; 🕑 noon-3pm & 7-10pm Tue-Sun; 🚊 Lido
Keeping it real on the Lido, this local hang-out serves respectable *cicheti* (Venetian tapas) and decent pizza at fair prices to a regular happy-hour crowd. If movie stars drop by, well, that can't be helped – after all, this is the handiest pizzeria to the Palazzo della Cinema.

🍴 TRATTORIA ANDRI
Classic Venetian €€€
☎ 041 5265482; Via Lepanto 21; 🕑 1.30-4pm Wed-Sun; 🚊 Lido
While others tan midday away, foodies head for a leisurely lunch at this canalside restaurant. The menu at Trattoria Andri focuses on simply prepared seafood: shrimp salad, grilled fish and *fritto misto* (fried seafood). Wash

BIKING THE LIDO

Stretch your legs and see more of the Lido on a bike, available by the hour or day at the self-evidently named **Lido on Bike** (☎ 041 5268019; www.lidoonbike.it; Gran Viale 21b; bike per hr single/tandem/double/family €3/6/7/14, bike per day single/tandem 9/18; 🕑 9am-7pm Mar-Oct; 🚊 Lido). This friendly bike-rental shop right near the Lido vaporetto (city-ferry) stop has reasonable prices and a map thrown in gratis. You must have official identification showing you're at least 18 to rent a bike.

Reserve a bike for the whole day so you don't have to rush – that'd defeat the whole point of laid-back Lido. For an easy loop that takes a couple of hours, start at the Lido vaporetto stop and head 3km south along the tree-lined, beachfront Lungomare Guglielmo Marconi to Malamocco (p135), where you can explore a miniature version of Venice. Mind the traffic – after a couple of days in pedestrian-only Venice, it's easy to forget the rules of the road. Then head back along Lungomare Guglielmo Marconi – braking for beauty, beaches and gelato like a local – and hang a left after the Palazzo della Cinema (p135) onto Via Quattro Fontane. Take a right along the canal onto Via S Giovanni d'Acri, which turns into winding Via Lepanto; make a pit stop for lunch at Trattoria Andri (p135), or take Gran Viale Santa Maria Elisabetta to Aurora Beach Club (opposite) to flop on a four-poster beach bed.

it down with well-priced wines and homemade sorbets, then see if you can make it back to that beach chair.

🍴 TRATTORIA LA FAVORITA
Classic Venetian €€
☎ 041 5261626; Via Francesco Duodo 33; 🕑 6-10pm Tue, noon-3.30pm & 7.30-11pm Wed-Sun, closed Jan–mid-Feb; 🚊 Lido
Spider-crab gnochetti, fish risotto and mixed *crudi* (composed bites of raw fish), all at noncelebrity prices, make La Favorita live up to its name. You should book ahead for the breezy, wisteria-filled garden – it's always a hot spot for visiting movie moguls and stubborn songbirds who aren't about

to be outdone by all those mobile-phone rings.

🍸 DRINK

🍸 COLONY BAR *Lounge*
☎ 041 5265921; Hotel des Bains, Lungomare Guglielmo Marconi 17; 🕑 9am-1am; 🚊 Lido
Celeb-spotting and cocktails on a historic Liberty-style verandah that's elegantly secluded by maritime pines – ah, this is Lido living. Your drink tab will easily match your cabana rental for the day, but you'll enjoy all the five-star perks – fawning service, top-shelf hooch, even lobby wi-fi access – without paying the Hotel des Bains room rate.

PLAY

AURORA BEACH CLUB
Beach Club, DJs

☎ 041 5268013; www.aurora.st;
Lungomare Gabriele D'Annunzio 20x;
🕙 9am-2am May-Sep; 🚹 Lido

After a long day relaxing and unwinding on a lounger, there's nothing better than relaxing and unwinding on a carved four-poster beach bed. Days flow into nights at this venue, aided by diversions such as free books and magazines, beach-sport and chill-out zones, live-music sets, cocktail bars, an open-air cinema and DJ sets that will keep you on the dance floor until you face plant on the sofa.

MULTISALA ASTRA *Cinema*

☎ 041 5265736; Via Corfu 9; adult/student/senior €7/4/5; 🕙 shows 5pm, 6pm, 8pm & 9.15pm; 🚹 Lido

When you start feeling the burn on the beach, catch a show at this dark, air-conditioned cinema instead. The program is planned by the Venice municipal film commission, which makes sure there are art-house options alongside blockbusters.

ULTIMA SPIAGGIA DI PACHUKA *Beach Club, DJs*

off Map p133; ☎ 348 3968466; Viale V Klinger, Spiaggia San Nicolò; admission €20; 🕙 noon-11pm; 🚹 San Nicolò

This place has all the sand of the Lido and all the laid-back boardwalk attitude of the Zattere, plus beer, pizza, and space for emerging artists among the beach umbrellas. Live music starts at 10pm on Fridays, while disco hits the beach with DJ sets on Saturdays.

>THE LAGOON

Other cities have suburban sprawl and malls – Venice has a teal blue lagoon dotted with photogenic islands and rare wildlife. Sometimes separated only by narrow channels, the city's outlying islands range from celebrated glass centres and a former Byzantine capital to deserted nunneries and garden isles. Serious shoppers hop the vaporetto (city ferry) to Murano, snapping up limited-edition glass pieces created with techniques that have been used since the 8th century; escapists prefer lazy days spent boating on the lagoon. Spot mohawked storks balancing thoughtfully on one leg and cormorants holding their wings out to dry after a fish dinner, then head to the fishing isle of Burano to get your own seafood meal amid a cheerful riot of colour-saturated houses. The golden mosaics at Torcello's Cattedrale di Santa Maria Assunta end lagoon adventures on a heavenly note.

Become enlightened on Murano (p141), where too much glass is never enough

BURANO & TORCELLO (p140)

Torcello

Burano

Mazzorbo

Isola di San Francesco del Deserto

Sant'Erasmo

Isola della Madonna del Monte

Isola Buel del Lovo

Isola di San Giacomo in Palude

Punta Sabbioni

Via Fausta

Punta Sabbioni

Lido di Treporti

Cavallino

Litorale di San Erasmo

Idroscalo Sant'Andrea

Lido di Venezia

Isola di San Andrea

Punta Longa

Isola Carbonera

Le Vignole

Isola La Certosa

MURANO (p142)

Murano

Isola di San Michele

Isola di Tessera

Sacca Serenella

Cimitero

VENICE

Isola di San Giorgio Maggiore

Isola di San Servolo

Isola di San Lazzaro degli Armeni

Isola la Grazia

Isola di San Clemente

Isola di Campalto

Isola di San Secondo

Isola della Giudecca

Sacca Fisola

SS11

Via Orlanda

SS11

Isola del Tronchetto

Ponte della Libertà

Isola di Tresse

Isola di San Giorgio in Alga

Isola di Sant'Angelo

Martiri della Libertà

Fusina

0   1   2 km

0   1 mile

SESTIERI

THE LAGOON

👁 SEE
🎨 BURANO

Map p140; 🚤 Burano, Mazzorbo

Strip away Venice's monumental overdose on Gothic ornamentation and crank up the colour palette from pastel to punchy, and there you have the charming island of Burano, located a 40-minute ferry ride from San Marco. Come for the colours, then stay for the cookies: Burano's vaguely lemony, crumbling ring- and S-shaped biscuits are ideal for dunking in dessert wines. Burano was traditionally famous for its lace, but at the time of writing the Museo di Merletto (Lace Museum) was closed for restoration and much of the lace for sale in Buranelli boutiques was imported; be sure to ask for a guarantee of authenticity if you're buying. When lace-crazed tour groups descend on the island, cross the wooden bridge to neighbouring Mazzorbo to find plenty of green space, a playground and a seemingly sacrilegious public toilet in the apse of a former chapel. See p24 for more on Burano.

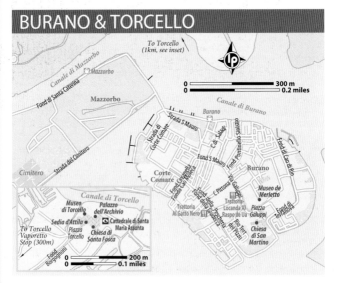

BURANO & TORCELLO

VENICE BY BOAT

Viewing the city and its lagoon by boat is an essential Venetian experience. A trip on a gondola or a vaporetto (city ferry) are two options, but if you want something a bit different try one of the following options.

Sail away into the lagoon blue in a Venetian *sampierota*, an elegant twin-sailed boat that's small enough to slip into canals but sturdy enough to glide across open water. The boats run by **Laguna Eco Adventures** (☎ 329 7226289; www.lagunaecoadventures.com; tour €30-120) accommodate a maximum of five people, so it's just you, the lagoon birds and the wind at your backs. Customised itineraries range from a circuit of outlying lagoon islands to an easy drift along the backstreets of Venice at sunset. Reserve ahead and, since all trips are subject to weather conditions, check weather forecasts.

The skipper at **Terra e Acqua** (☎ 347 4205004; www.terraeacqua.com; tour incl lunch €70-120), Cristina della Toffola (p143), is a wealth of information about rare lagoon wildlife, and has all sorts of juicy historical titbits, including stories of scandalous nunneries in Venice's notorious baroque party era. Itineraries are customised, and can cover abandoned plague quarantine islands, fishing and bird-watching hot spots, Burano, Torcello and other lagoon architectural gems. Cristina makes a mean fish stew and *spritz* (prosecco-based cocktail), which are served on board at picturesque island mooring spots; she also takes the utmost care to preserve the fragile lagoon ecosystem en route. Up to 10 people can be accommodated on Cristina's sturdy *bragosso* (Venetian barge), which makes the trip both sociable and easier going for those not accustomed to boats. Reserve well ahead and bring your sunscreen.

◉ MURANO

Brick warehouses and industrial smokestacks disguise the combustible creativity held within Murano's glass studios and showrooms. Hear the eerie heavy breathing of furnaces along the *fondamente* (canal banks) and follow the red glow into studios to glimpse glass-blowing in progress. For shoppers, however, the main attraction of Murano is obvious: the showrooms, where prices for hand-blown original glassworks are as good as they're going to get.

◉ MURANO COLLEZIONI

Map p142; ☎ 041 736272; Fondamenta Manin 1c-d; ⏱ 10am-5pm Tue-Sun; 🚋 Colonna

Like divas at La Fenice, the signature glass pieces in this darkened brick warehouse show perfect poise on their elegantly spotlighted pedestals. Famed Murano glass-designers Barovier&Toso, Carlo Moretti and Venini are all represented here, and even if you're not in the market for such high-end glass you're welcome to admire their luminous designs.

SESTIERI

THE LAGOON

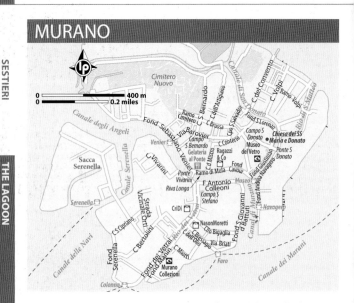

MURANO

MUSEO DEL VETRO

Museum of Glass; Map p142; ☎ 041
739586; www.museiciviciveneziani
.it; 8 Fondamenta Giustinian; adult/EU
6-14yr, student & over 65yr €5.50/3,
with Museum pass or VeniceCard free;
🕐 10am-6pm Thu-Tue Apr-Oct, 10am-
4pm Nov-Mar, ticket office closes 1hr
earlier; 🚊 Museo

Centuries ago, glass-blowers who
left Murano risked assassination;
since 1861, however, Murano has
shared its secrets and major in-
novations at the Museo del Vetro.
Roman glass from the 3rd century

AD is featured alongside clever
postmodern works, including Maria
Grazia Rosin's 1992 spray bottle
and detergent jug, both made from
impeccably blown glass. Upstairs
there's an explanation of how glass
is made, including a discussion
of the technique used to create
Venetian trade beads. Across the
hall are 17th-century baroque
glass triumphs such as winged
goblets, plus Carlo Scarpa's 1930
octopus and Romano Chirivi's 1968
Inutili (Useless) wineglasses, which
require drinking straws.

Cristina della Toffola
Terra e Acqua (p141) captain and lagoon naturalist

Seafaring DNA My family has boats in common – one brother is a gondola-maker [at Squero di San Trovaso, p115] and the other is a gondolier. We collaborate, but anyway, they're my younger brothers, so they can't boss me around. *[laughs]* **How many times she's fallen into canals** Venetians never fall into canals! OK, maybe once, when I slipped helping someone on board. No big deal, just unpleasant. A canal isn't a swimming pool, and it doesn't smell like one either – so watch your step, especially after a *spritz* [prosecco-based cocktail]. **Lagoon birds to spot** Storks, cormorants, kingfishers and black terns, which Venetians call *cocal* after the sound they make. **Yours, mine, ours** Unesco is right. Venice doesn't belong just to Venetians; it's a treasure that belongs to the whole world. Looking after it is easy if everyone does their part. Don't litter, don't speed in boats, and proceed carefully in fragile lagoon wildlife areas.

SESTIERI

THE LAGOON

◉ TORCELLO

This wild island was once Ernest Hemingway's favourite hunting ground, but its true claim to fame is as a former capital of Byzantium. From the vaporetto stop it's a 10-minute stroll past lagoon ducks and sheep pens to the charmingly overgrown central piazza, which contains a small museum and antiques shop. But across this square is the real treasure: the Cattedrale di Santa Maria Assunta. See p24 for more on Torcello.

◉ CATTEDRALE DI SANTA MARIA ASSUNTA

Map p140; ☎ 041 296 0630; Piazza Torcello; church/church & museum €4/6; ⏱ **10.30am-6pm Mar-Oct, 10am-5pm Nov-Feb, last entry 30min earlier;** 🏛 **Torcello**

At this mesmerising medieval church, life choices are presented as a mosaic cautionary tale: look ahead to a golden afterlife with the beatific Madonna gleaming in the apse, or turn your back on her and face the blue devil gloating over skewered souls and skulls squirming with worms. If time permits, climb the bell tower (last entry one hour before closing time) for views of the lagoon, or browse Roman bronzes and stone relics from Torcello's Byzantine heyday at the quirky little museum across the piazza.

Medieval visions of hell at the Cattedrale di Santa Maria Assunta

🛍 SHOP
🛍 MURANO
🛍 CRIDI *Glass*
Map p142; ☎ 041 5275379; Fondamenta dei Vetrai 116; ⏱ 9am-1pm & 3-5.30pm Mon-Sat; 🚏 Colonna

Rings are the thing at CriDi, where the owners – a couple who are both Murano glass designers – have packed the shelves with handmade, portable gift possibilities in the €15 to €75 range. Most jewellery pieces here are created using lampwork techniques, where glass rods are carefully fused together with a hand-held blowtorch into patterns that range from starbursts to psychedelic swirls. Check out the chic cold-worked rings, which are made from glass that has been carefully sculpted after it has cooled.

🛍 NASONMORETTI *Glass*
Map p142; ☎ 041 5274866; www.nasonmoretti.com; Fondamenta Manin 52; ⏱ 10am-6pm Mon-Sat; 🚏 Colonna

Unexpected asymmetrical shapes and striking two-colour combinations have been the trademark of these modernist masters since the 1950s; today NasonMoretti's third-generation glass designers are layering heavy crystal over coloured glass to create vases that look like pure liquid colour trapped in ice. Prices start at a surprisingly

reasonable €31 for signed hand-blown drinking glasses, but with growing interest from museums in the US, don't expect the deals to last forever.

🛍 RAGAZZI & CO *Glass*
Map p142; ☎ 041 736818; Ramo di Mula 16; ⏱ 9.30am-5.30pm Mon-Sat; 🚏 Museo

A Klimt painting melted into a plate, a tiny lagoon trapped under glass, ink spilled onto a polka-dot glass vase…such leaps of the imagination are the speciality of this Murano glass designer. The signature bullseye design here is a clever abstraction of traditional Muranese *millefiori* (thousand-flower) patterns, with bullseyes clustering by the hundreds on tiny oval plates and square steel-topped key rings. Starting at €38, prices are reasonable for the work.

🍴 EAT
🍴 BURANO
🍴 TRATTORIA AL GATTO NERO *Classic Venetian* €€€
Map p140; ☎ 041 730120; www.gattonero.com; Via Giudecca 88; ⏱ noon-3.30pm & 7.30-9.30pm Tue-Sun; 🚏 Burano

Italian foodies, movie stars and dignitaries have taken such a shine to this Burano restaurant that reservations are now

Discover an eye for colour on picture-perfect Burano (p140)

necessary in this out-of-the-way spot. But once you've tried the homemade tagliolini with spider crab, risotto with langoustine, ultrafresh grilled fish and perfect house-baked Burano biscuits, a phone call – or even a swim from Venice – seems like a minor effort to make for such a major meal. This is a good place to opt for canalside seating, because you won't be neglected; meals are served efficiently, with pleasant banter in English and a proud Buranesi flourish.

🍴 TRATTORIA-LOCANDA AL RASPO DE UA
Classic Venetian   €€
Map p140; ☎ 041 730095; www.alraspo deua.it; Piazza Galuppi 560; 🚹 Burano

Lazy lunches alongside the piazza let you watch the lace-shopping frenzy from a safe distance. Try a plate of delicate prawn pasta, made in the sparkling clean, hyperefficient kitchen, then linger over vin santo and S-shaped Buranesi biscuits.

🍴 MURANO
🍴 GELATERIA AL PONTE
Gelato, Sandwiches   €
Map p142; ☎ 041 736278; Riva Longa 1c; 🕐 9am-5pm Mon-Sat; 🚹 Museo
Toasted prosciutto-and-cheese *panini* (sandwiches; €3 to €5) and gelato (€2) give shoppers their second wind without cutting into Murano glass-buying budgets. Table service can be slow, so order at the bar if you're in a rush.

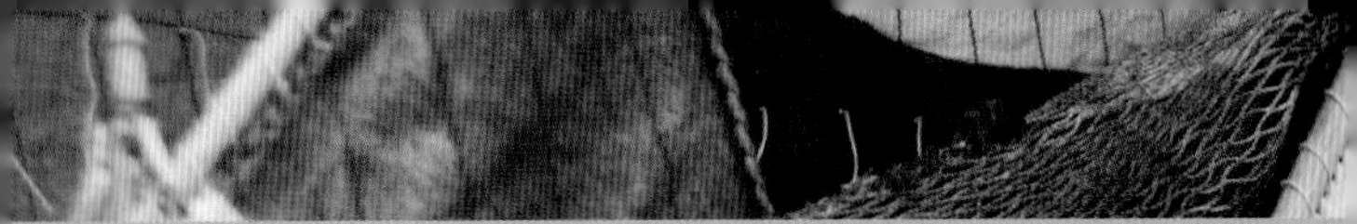

>SNAPSHOTS

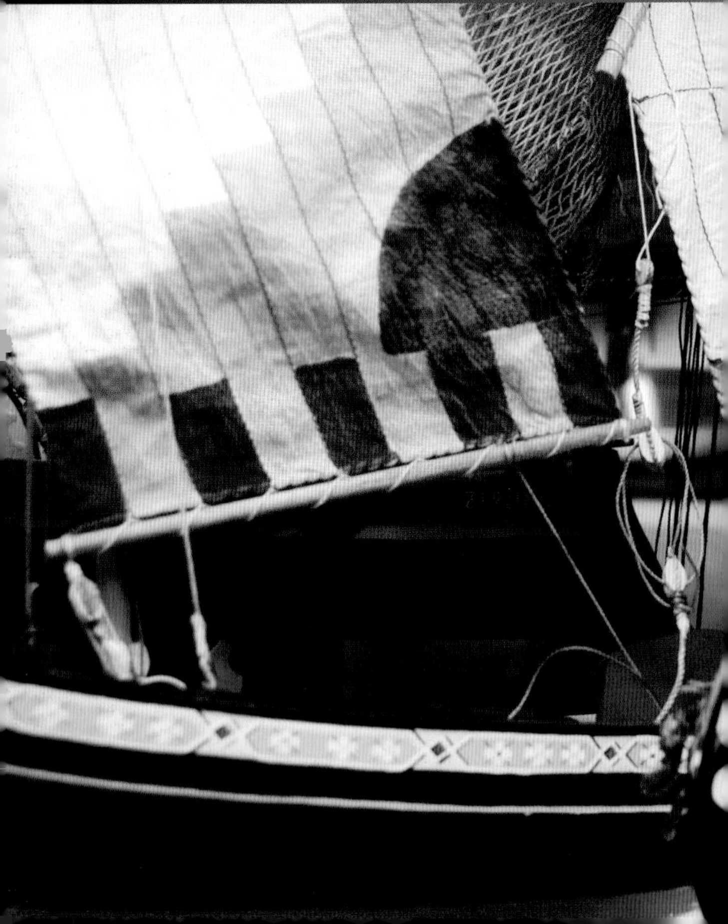

Bliss is never more than a bridge and a couple of *calli* (streets) away in Venice, but here are a few pointers to get you there that much faster.

Gilberto Penzo (p88): a model boat builder?

ACCOMMODATION

First things first: you do not have to stay on the mainland, missing the opportunity to wake up in fairy-tale Venice. Whoever keeps circulating the rumour that Venice doesn't have enough beds offers no rooms under €200 is about a decade out of date – and hasn't heard of the internet.

Over the past 10 years, many Venetians have opened their homes as B&Bs or *affittacamere* (rooms for rent). These places are much more personable than Venice's big hotels, and they're often tucked away in neighbourhoods where you can mingle with the locals but still be close to the sights. Better still, you can compare costs online, then negotiate a rate that fits your budget by emailing the hotel or B&B directly. Compare hotels, B&Bs and apartments at www.veniceby.com; consider more B&B options at www.bed-and-breakfast.it; and find still more apartments and B&Bs at www.slowtrav.com/italy. If that isn't enough choice, the Azienda di Promozione Turistica (APT) lists more than 250 *affittacamere* and B&Bs at www.turismovenezia.it. With research, you can find places that don't double their low-season price in high season, and even a few places under €100.

If you're still thinking of staying in Mestre, consider the following scenario. You stay in Venice until sundown to get the full effect of this romantic city, linger over a *spritz* (prosecco-based cocktail), then decide you'll try a promising Venetian *osteria* (restaurant-bar) you read about in this book (clever you). After a lovely meal, you have to catch a train to Mestre; even if your hotel is in a nice part of town, the train station certainly isn't. Tomorrow, instead of waking up to the sound of gondoliers crying 'Oooooeee!', you've got a symphony of honks at Mestre rush hour.

So, that being said: where would you like to stay in Venice? The most reasonably priced B&Bs and *affitacamere* are clustered in residential sections of Santa Croce, San Polo and Cannaregio; B&Bs in San Marco, Dorsoduro and Castello, with proximity to major attractions, tend to be pricier. Dorsoduro and San Marco offer many chic boutique accommodations, Cannaregio is a good bet for quiet and period charm, and Santa Croce and Giudecca offer a Venetian immersion experience just off the tourist trail.

When nothing less than a *palazzo* (palace or mansion) with a Grand Canal view will do, you'll probably end up staying in San Marco. Several of the historic palaces along the Grand Canal have been bought by hotel chains, adding an air of brisk efficiency to these luxury operations that you'll find either helpful or off-putting. The Starwood-run Gritti Palace has maintained its swagger and antique charm, while the Monaco & Grand Canal Hotel – a former high-baroque gambling den – has recently completed an elegant renovation. For a luxury waterfront stay, you might also consider staying in a Palladio-designed cloister at the new Bauer Palladio & Spa or head to the Lido for the Liberty art deco grandeur of the Hotel des Bains.

BEST SPLURGES

> Bauer Palladio (www.palladiohotel spa.com)
> Monaco & Grand Canal Hotel (www.hotelmonaco.it)
> Gritti Palace (www.starwood hotels.com)
> Ca' Pisani (www.capisanihotel.it)
> Hotel des Bains (www.starwood hotels.com)

BEST DESIGNER B&BS

> Charming House DD.724 (www.the charminghouse.com)
> Palazzo Soderini (www.palazzo soderini.it)
> Ca' Pozzo (www.capozzoinn.com)
> Domus Orsoni (Domus Orsoni)
> Bloom/7 Cielo (www.bloom -venice.com)

BEST FOR PERIOD CHARM

> Hotel Flora (www.hotelflora.it)
> Pensione La Calcina (www.lacalcina .com)
> Locanda Barbarigo (www.locanda barbarigo.com)
> Casa Verardo (www.casaverardo.it)
> Ca' della Corte (www.cadellacorte.com)

BEST UNDER €100

> Pensione Guerrato (www.pension eguerrato.it)
> Foresteria Valdese (www.foresteria venezia.it)
> Hotel Aì Do Mori (www.hotelaido mori.com)
> Hotel dalla Mora (www.hoteldalla mora.it)
> Residenzia Junghans (www.residenza junghans.com)

GRAND CANAL

How grand is it, really? With some 50 palaces, six churches, four bridges, scene-stealing cameos in four James Bond films, two open-air markets and one rather picturesque prison (from the outside, anyway), this water-way definitely earns its name and fame. To get the full effect, travel the length of the Grand Canal at night, when dock lights turn into frenzied Tintoretto brush strokes on the water, and Murano chandeliers and Tiepolo ceilings can be glimpsed through *palazzo* windows.

To max out on romance, tour the Grand Canal by *sampierota* (narrow sailboat) or gondola at night. During the day, *motoschiaffi* (motor boats) whiz past and kick up wakes that upset smaller crafts and wear away the *fondamente* (canal banks) of the Grand Canal, much to the dismay of Venetians in general, but especially of gondolieri, who can get grumpy when asked to take the Grand Canal. So unless you have a yacht and filming clearance – like Daniel Craig in *Casino Royale* – vaporetto (city ferry) 1 is your best bet to cover the Grand Canal by day. With a 12-hour vaporetto ticket, you can hop on and off wherever you like en route to San Marco. Embark at the train station, and as you chug up the canal, keep an eye out for the following landmarks.

On the right, the baroque Baldassare Longhena–designed Ca' Pesaro (p99) juts out into the canal. Housing a modern-art gallery and the Museo Orientale, this *palazzo* has a deep double arcade atop a faceted marble base, and chiselled good looks to rival any Bond.

The next vaporetto stop on your left is the Venetian Gothic Ca' d'Oro (p71), with two tiers of peekaboo quatrefoil portholes lightly balancing atop lacy arcades. Beauty queen that it is, the Ca' d'Oro is capped with crenulation that looks like a tiara. Hop off here to check out Andrea Mantegna's magnificent *St Sebastian* and other Napoleonic plunder.

In the morning, you'll hear the Rialto produce markets (p94) and covered Pescheria (p94) before you see them on your right. Fishmongers call out the catch of the day in Venetian dialect, and vendors brag shamelessly about their artichokes. If your stomach's growling, there's a vaporetto stop here. Otherwise, continue under the Ponte di Rialto (p86), watching tourists hanging off the side of the bridge like gargoyles to get the best photo.

As you round the next bend, the splendid Longhena-designed Ca' Rezzonico (p109) will be on your right, with two stories of grand window arcades to shed natural light on the Tiepolo ceilings inside. Hop off at the vaporetto stop out front to binge on baroque art here.

Staring down the Ca' Rezzonico from across the canal is the Palazzo Grassi (p47), recently resuscitated by billionaire François Pinault with minimalist architect Tadao Ando. The front dock is a contemporary sculpture installation featuring floating conversation pieces such as Subodh Gupta's giant skull made of cooking pots. To see the Grassi's latest show, disembark at the next stop at the Ponte dell'Accademia (p113).

Keeping a low profile on the right bank is the Peggy Guggenheim Collection (p113). Look for the Alexander Calder by the dock, and peek between the shrubs for Marino Marini's 1948 *Angel of the City,* a nude figure on a horse who is apparently very excited indeed by this view of the Grand Canal. For a closer look, get off at the next vaporetto stop in front of the Chiesa di Santa Maria della Salute (p112). Shrouded in semipermanent restoration efforts and a certain mystery, this unusual octagonal shrine echoes Roman temples to Venus and mystical cabbala diagrams. Alight here to see early Titians, or press on past the Punta della Dogana (p114).

End your Grand Canal tour near Piazza San Marco at the San Zaccaria stop, passing the Ducal Palace (p45) on your left and entering the Prigioni Nuove (New Prisons) just in time for your evening jazz concert (p69).

Top left Take in the grand view from the Ponte dell'Accademia (p113)

FOOD

Local Food! may be the latest foodie motto, but it's nothing new in Venice. Surrounded by garden islands and a lagoon's worth of seafood, Venice offers local specialities that never make it to the mainland, because the produce is all served fresh the same day in Venetian *bacari* (bars) and *osterie*. But Venice's cosmopolitan outlook must also be credited with keeping the city ahead of the foodie curve. After making an art of traditional Venetian recipes like *sarde in saor* (sardines in an onion marinade) and *baccalà mantecato* (mashed cod prepared in garlic and parsley), Venetian cooks are reinventing them with spice-route flavours from Venice's trading past. The occasional exceptional ingredient from another part of Italy sneaks in, such as Tuscan beef fillets and Sicilian blood oranges – but only in moderation.

Luckily for you, there's still room at the bar to score the best *cicheti* (Venetian tapas), and reservations are still readily available for phenomenal eateries. Stories about how it's impossible to eat well and economically in Venice have circulated for decades, misinforming day trippers clinging defensively to their pizza slices in San Marco. Little do they realize that for the same price they could be dining on crostini topped with scampi and grilled baby artichoke, or tuna tartare with wild strawberries and a balsamic reduction.

Once you know what to look for, Venice becomes a foodie treasure hunt. Beware any menu dotted with asterisks indicating that items are *surgelati* (frozen). Lasagne, spaghetti Bolognese and pizza are not Venetian specialities, so avoid any tourist trap where all three appear on the menu. Look for places where there's no menu at all, or one hastily scrawled on a chalkboard or laser-printed in Italian only. This is a sign your chef reinvents the menu daily according to what's on offer at the market.

Your favourite meals may be eaten standing up at 6.30pm, the moment *cicheti* are put out at many *bacari*. However, you should treat yourself to one leisurely sit-down meal while you're in Venice, whether it's in a back-alley *osteria* or a canalside restaurant. You'll win over your waiter and the chef by doing the following:

Ignore the menu. Solicit your server's advice about seasonal treats and house specials, pick two options that sound interesting, and ask your server to recommend one over the other. When that's done, snap the menu shut and say, '*Allora, facciamo cosi, per favore!*' (Well then, let's do that, please!) You have just made your waiter's day and flattered the chef.

Drink well. Bottled water is optional (local *acqua al rubinetto,* tap water, is perfectly drinkable) but fine meals call for wine, which is often available by the glass or half bottle. Don't worry if you don't recognise the label; the best small-production local wineries don't advertise or export, because their entire yield is snapped up by Venetian *osterie.*

Try primi *(first courses) without condiments.* Your waiter's relief and delight will be obvious – Venetian seafood pastas are rich and flavourful enough without being smothered in Parmesan or hot sauce.

Go with local seafood. No one expects you to order an appetiser or *secondo piatto* (second course), but if you do, the tests of any Venetian chef are fish antipasti and *frittura* (fried seafood). Try yours *senza limone* (without lemon) first; Venetians believe the delicate flavours of their seafood are best complimented by salt and pepper.

BEST CICHETI
> All'Arco (p91)
> Osteria I Rusteghi (p54)
> Alla Vedova (p77)
> Un Mondo di Vino (p80)
> Pronto Pesce Pronto (p94)

BEST INVENTIVE VENETIAN
> Anice Stellato (p77)
> Osteria di Santa Marina (p68)
> Al Fontego dei Pescatori (p77)
> Vecio Fritolin (p106)
> I Figli delle Stelle (p130)

BEST TRADITIONAL VENETIAN
> Al Covo (p66)
> Ristorante Cantinone Storico (p120)
> Ristoteca Oniga (p120)
> Trattoria al Gatto Nero (p145)
> Vini da Gigio (p79)

BEST SPECIALITY JOINTS
> Alaska Gelateria (p104) for gelato
> La Bitta (p120) for meat
> Osteria La Zucca (p106) for veggie dishes
> Pasticceria Gobbetti (p120) for chocolate treats
> Vini da Arturo (p54) for steaks

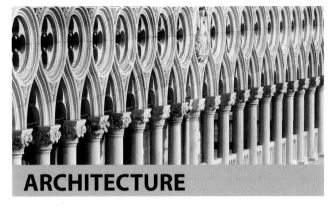

ARCHITECTURE

Lulls in conversation in Venice are easily resolved with one innocent question: what is Venetian architecture? Venice's cosmopolitan flair defines its architecture, from the 7th- and 9th-century Byzantine Cattedrale di Santa Maria Assunta (p144) on Torcello to Tadao Ando's 2008 reinvention of the Punta della Dogana customs houses (p114). An East–West landmark that defies any single genre, the Basilica di San Marco (p41) covers every style from Byzantine Constantinople to 19th-century Renaissance revival. In contrast, Venice's Gothic I Frari (p84), Zanipolo (p64) and Chiesa della Maria dell'Orto (p74) are actually more austere than their French cousins. The Venetian Renaissance revived classical ideas under Jacopo Sansovino (1486–1570) and Andrea Palladio (1508–80), who combined classical geometry with a generous baroque sense of interior space in Chiesa di San Giorgio Maggiore (p126) and Il Redentore (p128). But just when Venetian architecture began to seem set in its classicising ways, Baldassare Longhena (1598–1682) redefined 17th-century baroque with his Roman-and-cabbala-inspired Chiesa di Santa Maria della Salute (p112).

Everyone has a pet period in Venice's chequered architectural history. Ruskin waxed rhapsodic about Byzantine Gothic Basilica di San Marco, and detested Palladio and his Chiesa di San Giorgio Maggiore; Palladians rebuffed rococo; fans of the regal rococo of Ca' Rezzonico were scandalised by the Lido's bohemian Liberty style; and pretty much everyone was horrified by the inclinations of industry to strip Venice of its ornamentation.

After Giudecca's baroque buildings were torn down for factories, the city took decades to recover from the shock. Architects reverted to venezianitá, a tendency to tack on to buildings exaggerated Venetian elements from a range of periods – a Gothic trefoil arch here, a baroque cupola there. Rather than using the interiors of the buildings to harmonise these disparate architectural elements, Venetians swagged them in silk damask and lit them with Murano chandeliers. The resulting hotchpotch seemed to signal the end of Venice's architectural glory days.

Then came the flood of 1966, and it seemed all of Venice's architectural patrimony would be lost. Architecture aficionados around the globe put aside their differences, and aided Venetians to bail out *palazzi* and reinforce foundations across the city. With preservation efforts and postmodernism came a fresh approach to Venice's composite architecture; rather than tearing down one style or wallpapering over differences, architects chose spare modern treatments to creatively repurpose the past. With this approach, the Fondazione Giorgio Cini converted a naval academy into a gallery, while Tadao Ando has turned the Punta della Dogana customs houses into a contemporary-art showplace.

BEST ARCHITECTURAL LANDMARKS
> Basilica di San Marco (p41)
> Chiesa di San Giorgio Maggiore (p126)
> Ducal Palace (p45)
> Chiesa di Santa Maria dei Miracoli (p74)
> Chiesa di Santa Maria della Salute (p112)

BEST MODERN ARCHITECTURE
> Palazzo Grassi (p47)
> Biennale pavilions (p59)
> Fondazione Querini Stampalia (p59)
> Fondazione Giorgio Cini (p127)
> Punta della Dogana (p114)

Top left Gorgeously Gothic Ducal Palace (p45) **Above** A healthy sense of proportion at Chiesa di Santa Maria della Salute (p112)

SNAPSHOTS

ARTISANS

It may be hard to describe your Venice souvenirs without sounding like you're bragging. 'It's an original,' you'll say, 'and I met the artisan.' While artisanal traditions across the rest of the industrialised world have disappeared or been fossilised into relics of bygone eras, Venetians have kept their craft tradition alive, innovative and surprisingly accessible.

From clever *carta marmorizzata* (marbled-paper) travel journals (€12) to custom-made red-carpet shoes (€200), Venice's handcrafted goods are reasonably priced for the labour involved; costs are competitive with mass-produced merchandise that has logos in lieu of individual personality. Paris' latest It bags seem uninspired compared to Venetian purses made from marbled paper or silk-screened velvet, and Tiffany jewellery seems ho-hum once you've glimpsed the glass-ring selection in Murano.

So how did you come by that Venetian heirloom piece, you crafty shopper? First you had to know where to look: down the back alleys of San Polo, Santa Croce, Dorsoduro, San Marco, Castello and Murano, and inside the studios and showrooms of local artisans. Studios tend to cluster together, so getting lost in an artisans' area is a great way to find unique pieces. Showrooms filled with glass and shelves of fragile handicrafts may be labelled *Non Toccare* (Don't Touch) – instead of risking breakage, just ask the staff to show you the pieces. The person who shows it to you may be the very person who made it, so don't be shy about saying *'Complimenti!'* (My compliments!) for impressive pieces. In a world of knock offs and cookie-cutter culture, your support for these handicrafts is a vote for Venice's enduring originality.

BEST VENICE ORIGINALS
> Book-bound handbags at Cartè (p87)
> Enamelled skull earrings at Sigfrido Cipolato (p66)
> Hand-stamped recipe books at Il Pavone (p117)
> *Forcole* at Pastor (p118)
> Sea-anemone bracelets at Gualti (p115)

BEST GLASS DESIGNS
> Glass-studded necklaces at Marina e Susanna Sent (p117)
> Liquid-crystal vases at NasonMoretti (p145)
> Glass mosquitoes at I Vetri a Lume di Amadi (p89)
> Bullseye glass plates at Ragazzi & Co (p145)
> Glass rings at CriDi (p145)

MUSIC & OPERA

Over the centuries, Venetian musicians developed a reputation for playing music as though their lives depended on it – which at times wasn't that far from the truth. In its heyday, Venice had official musicians and distinct party music, but it was only when it fell on hard times in the 17th and 18th centuries that it really discovered its musical talents. With shrinking trade revenues, the state took the rather quixotic step of underwriting the musical education of orphan girls, and the investment yielded extraordinary returns. Visitors to the city spread word of superb performances by the girls, and Venice's reputation for music made it a magnet for socialites.

Today's televised talent searches can't compare to Venice's ability to discover musical talents, including Claudio Monteverdi, who was named the musical director of the Basilica di San Marco and went on to launch modern opera. Similarly, one of the maestri hired to conduct the orphan-girl orchestras was Antonio Vivaldi, who in the course of his 30-year tenure wrote hundreds of concertos and popularised Venetian music across Europe.

Modern visitors to Venice can still see music performed in much the same venues as it was in Vivaldi's day – *palazzi,* churches and *ospedaletti* (orphanages). But rather than playing classical music or opera as period pieces, Venice's leading interpreters perform with verve and wit, keeping up their end of a musical conversation that began centuries ago.

BEST PERFORMANCES & VENUES

> Teatro La Fenice (p57)
> Interpreti Veneziani (p97) at Scuola Grande di San Rocco
> Jazz in Venice (p69) in Prigioni Nuove
> Musica a Palazzo (p56) in Palazzo Barbarigo-Minotto
> Venice Chamber Music Orchestra at Ca' Rezzonico (p109)

BEST MUSICAL MEMENTOS

> CDs and music appreciation books from Mondadori (p51)
> Harmonicas and flutes from Mille e Una Nota (p89)
> Clothes based on costumes worn by La Fenice divas from Banco 10 (p65)
> CDs from Parole e Musica (p65)
> Vivaldi biographies from Libreria Studium (p50)

V

SHOPPING

Churches and museums are all well and good, but who are we kidding? In Italy anyone with the faintest retail inclination is going to wind up in a store eventually. That doesn't mean you have to end up with one of those glittered porcelain-mask magnets or a striped gondolier shirt (though, hey, those can be quite hip out of context). In Venice you can find gifts by local artisans that truly are one of a kind; the odds of a work-mate showing up to the Christmas party in the same locally designed Fortuny frock or Fiorella smoking jacket are infinitesimal.

Mall shopping just can't compare to treasure hunting in Venice. Sure, there are the standard Italian designer brands along Via Larga XXII Marzo and Calle dei Fabbri in San Marco, but the rarest finds and sweetest deals await across the Grand Canal in the backstreet boutiques of San Polo and Dorsoduro. Open-air markets reveal hidden gems – exquisite enamelled lockets or an actual pirate's pipe – and at fair-trade boutiques your sun-hat purchase supports a worthy cause. Depending on your country's customs regulations, Venetian edibles and wines make tasteful souvenirs.

BEST FOR FASHION
> Fiorella Gallery (p48)
> Maliparmi (p50)
> Penny Lane Vintage (p103)
> Venetia Studium (p51)
> Hibiscus (p88)

BEST FEEL-GOOD RETAIL
> Banco 10 (p65)
> Venice's artisans (p158)
> Le Botteghe (p49)
> Acqua Altra (p115)
> Mercato delle pulci (p114)

BEST ART & ANTIQUES
> Caterina Tognon Arte (p44)
> Antichità Teresa Ballarin (p115)
> Galleria Traghetto (p45)
> Campiello Ca' Zen (p87)
> Mercantino dei Miracoli (p114)

BEST HOMEWARES
> Madera (p117)
> NasonMoretti (p145)
> Fortuny Tessuti Artistici (p128)
> Sabbie e Nebbie (p90)
> Epicentro (p48)

RELIGIOUS EXPERIENCES

After a few blissful days of wandering this fair city, the same thought occurs to most visitors: thank heaven for Venice. This is no coincidence. Soaring Venetian Gothic arches and rooftop synagogue cupolas direct the eye heavenward, museums are packed with masterpieces based on religious themes, and angels are in the architecture at street-corner shrines and *scuole* (religious confraternities). Venetians grateful for surviving plagues, floods and invasions showed their appreciation in monumental form, building 107 churches and seven synagogues where they could give thanks on a regular basis.

As if that weren't enough, pontoon bridges are strung across canals for festivals such as Festa del Redentore (p29) and Festa della Madonna della Salute (p30), when Venetians risk a dunking to light candles for the survival of their city. On saints' days – and at every opportunity – Venetians celebrate with sweet treats and toasts to the *bea vita* (good life).

With all this divine inspiration, where do you begin? Basilica di San Marco (p41) is an obvious choice, but the Museo delle Icone (p59) and the Museo Ebraico di Venezia (p75) show the diversity of Venice's religious traditions. Island retreats such as Chiesa di San Giorgio Maggiore (p126) show true devotion, but so do smaller neighbourhood institutions such as Chiesa di Santa Maria dei Miracoli (p74) and Chiesa di San Sebastian (p109).

BEST DIVINE INSPIRATIONS
> Mosaics at Basilica di San Marco (p41)
> *Madonna of the Assumption* at I Frari (p84)
> *The Last Judgment* at Chiesa della Madonna dell'Orto (p74)
> Longhena's stairway to heaven at Scuola Grande dei Carmini (p114)
> The women's gallery of the Spanish Scola synagogue (p75)

BEST HEAVENLY INDULGENCES
> Balsamic-vinegar chocolate truffles at Vizio Virtu (p91)
> *Zaete* (biscuits) and *krapfen* (doughnuts) at Festa della Madonna della Salute (p30)
> Mid-Biennale macchiato at Paradiso (p69)
> Pistachio gelato at Gelateria San Stae (p105)
> Prosecco and poetry at Sacro e Profano (p96)

SNAPSHOTS

OFF-SEASON VENICE

Winter is the most stirring movement of Vivaldi's *Four Seasons* for a reason – the composer had great source material. Just think of footsteps muffled by snow, icicles dripping from Venetian Gothic windows, and boots being stamped at the doorsteps of buzzing *bacari*. This is the season when Venetians let down their guard, bored chefs sit and chat over lunch, and artisans in their studios are glad of any interruption. Intrepid travellers may have Piazza San Marco to themselves as they skid across patches of ice in their rush to get to gooey hot chocolate.

There are also practical advantages to visiting Venice between November and March. Except at Christmas and Carnevale, prices are slashed on everything from accommodation and excursions to dinners and drinks. Museums have fewer visitors, and restaurants offer limited menus to mostly local crowds – which has a definite upside. Finally you can skip the queues and take in Titians at the Accademia and futurists at the Peggy Guggenheim Collection without meekly following the tour-group herds, then strike up conversations about Venetian colour over drinks afterwards.

BEST OFF-SEASON THINGS TO DO
> Learn Italian at Istituto Venezia (p121)
> Attend Biennale closing parties (p17)
> Cross the Grand Canal at Festa della Madonna della Salute (p30)
> Learn to cook Italian feasts with the Friends of Venice Club (p121)
> Celebrate Carnevale in costume at Teatro La Fenice (p57)

BEST SEASONAL SPECIALITIES
> *Anatra* (lagoon duck)
> *Moscardini* (baby octopus)
> *Granseola* (spider crab)
> *Radicchio di Treviso*
> *Fritole* (sweet fritters)

BEST OFF-SEASON TRAVEL ADVANTAGES
> Leisurely conversations with Venetians
> Last-minute tickets to La Fenice (p57)
> Reservations at the restaurant of your choice
> No lines at the Accademia (p113)
> Winter light inside San Marco (p41)

BEST WAYS TO STAY WARM
> Venetian hot chocolate
> *Brodo di pesce* (saffron-scented fish stew)
> *Pasta e fasioi* (pasta with beans)
> *Caffè corretto* (coffee 'corrected' with brandy)
> *Polenta umida* (soft polenta)

HANDS-ON VENICE

After you ogle your third Titian and 10th gondola, you may start to get ideas of your own. Technically you can't touch a Titian, and it takes years to become a gondolier, but the traditions of painting and boating are perfectly within reach. Even if gondolas and frescoes won't fit into your luggage, a model boat by Gilberto Penzo and paints from Arcobaleno might. Other souvenirs will pass even the toughest carry-on restrictions: an eye for colour developed at a printmaking workshop, an ear for baroque music discovered at a musical course, or a sense of balance lost and found the hard way through *voga alla veneta* (rowing standing up, Venetian style).

Inspiration is sprinkled across Venice, and it would be a shame to let it go to waste. Designing your own wine-tasting itinerary is easy: just connect the dots between the city's *enoteche* (wine bars) and *bacari*. Designing your own Carnevale costume is harder, but not impossible, while a cooking class (see www.venicevenetogourmet.com) will allow you to take Venetian happy hour home. If this city on the water has one standing lesson to offer, it's that imagination makes anything possible.

BEST THINGS TO TRY
> Capture Venice in moody aquatints at Bottega del Tintoretto (p81)
> Design your own Carnevale costume at Teatro Junghans (p131)
> Play a benefit concert with Friends of Venice Club (p121)
> Row across the Giudecca Canal with Maredicarta (p103)
> Learn mask-making secrets at Ca' Macana (p121)

BEST FOR DIY SUPPLIES
> Arcobaleno (p48) for art
> Maredicarta (p103) for sailing
> Gilberto Penzo (p88) for toy boats
> Drogheria Mascari (p87) for cooking
> Rialto produce markets (p94) for picnics and still-life paintings

V

CIN-CIN

No rules seem to apply to drinking in Venice. Happy hour from 6pm to 7pm? More like twice daily, from 11am to 3pm and 6.30pm to 8.30pm. No mixing spirits and wine? Venice's classic cocktails, such as *spritz* (made with prosecco, plus Aperol or Campari), suggest otherwise. No girly drinks? Tell that to burly boat builders enjoying a frothy prosecco.

This makes knowing what to order where a little tricky. Price is not an indicator of quality – you can pay €2 for a respectable *spritz,* or live to regret that €15 Bellini (ouch). If you're not pleased with your drink, leave it and move on to the next *bacaro*. Venice is too small and life too short to make do with ho-hum hooch.

In the rest of Italy, the DOC *(denominazione d'origine controllata)* and elite DOCG *(denominazione d'origine controllata e garantita)* designations are usually assurances of top-notch vino, but Veneto bucks the system. Several small-production Veneto wineries can't be bothered with such external validation, because they already sell out to Venetian *osterie* and *enoteche*. Even ordinary varietals take on extraordinary characteristics in the unusual Veneto growing regions, so a merlot or soave could be the most adventurous choice on the menu.

Happily, *osterie* and *enoteche* sell good stuff by the glass or half bottle, so you can discover new favourites without committing to a whole bottle. Even budding oenologists should solicit suggestions from *osterie* hosts, who'll accept the challenge of finding your new favourite Venetian tipple as a point of local pride. *Cin-cin* – bottoms up.

BEST VENETO WINES TO TRY

> Prosecco – the sparkling white that's the life of any Venetian party
> Refosco dal peduncolo rosso – intense and brooding
> Tocai – a dazzling, well-structured white worthy of Palladio
> Raboso del Piave – brash when young, brilliant with age
> Amarone – a profound, voluptuous red

BEST SIGNATURE DRINKS

> *Spritz* at Aurora Caffè (p56)
> Rialto at B Bar (p54)
> Morgana beer at La Cantina (p79)
> Bellini at Harry's Dolci (p130)
> Water bottles filled with wine from the barrel at Nave d'Oro (p95)

The Museo Storico Navale (p62) holds golden memories of Venice's glorious history

BACKGROUND

HISTORY

FROM SWAMP TO EMPIRE

A malarial swamp is a strange place to put a city – unless you're under attack by Huns and Goths. And so began the story of Venice in AD 452. Crafty settlers soon rose above their swampy circumstances, residing on land that was lifted above tides by wooden pylons driven into some 30m of soft silt.

Once terra firma was established, Venice set about shoring up its business interests. While rival Genoa was busy charting routes to the New World, Venice concentrated on controlling the last leg of the spice and silk trade routes to Europe. Jealous Genoa tried to take over the city and its maritime trade in 1380, after Venice was weakened by the plague. But Venice prevailed, and the city soon controlled a backyard that stretched from Dalmatia to Bergamo.

By the mid-15th century, Venice was swathed in golden mosaics and rustling silks, and doused in incense to cover the belching sulphuric smells that were the downside of a lagoon empire. La Serenissima (the Most Serene) retained its calm during this time with a complex system of checks and balances, plus bouts of outright repression: the Great Council elected a doge to preside over council matters, while Venice's shadowy secret service, the Consiglio dei Dieci (Council of Ten), thwarted conspiracies with a network of spies.

TRENDSETTERS AND TROUBLEMAKERS

As Venice lost ground to pirates and Ottomans, the city again rose to the occasion, conquering Europe by charm instead. Venice's art was

BETTER THAN BOND

Venice made a killing in the Crusades as a triple agent, accepting a Frankish commission of 84,000 silver marks to wrest the Holy Land from Muslim control, but continuing to trade with Muslim powers from Syria to Spain. But when the balance of the Frankish commission wasn't forthcoming, Venice decided to claim Constantinople with the aid of the Franks. While the city was ostensibly claimed for Christendom, Venice also benefited: ships loaded with booty were sent back home.

ROXANNE, YOU *DO* HAVE TO PUT OUT THE RED LIGHT

Venetian courtesans were widely admired taste makers and poets in the 14th century, so the city's idea of a crackdown was to decree that ladies of the night should have red lights attached to their gondolas, and should only display their wares in windows from the waist up rather than baring all in the streets. By the end of the 16th century, the town was flush with some 12,000 registered prostitutes, creating a literal red-light district. Today, however, red beacons mostly signal construction – but you can enjoy a decadent dinner at Antica Carampane (the Old Streetwalkers; p92), near Ponte delle Tette (Tits Bridge).

incredibly daring, bringing sensuous colour and sly social commentary to familiar religious subjects, while Venetian music (p159) was irresistibly catchy, instigating a merry mingling of men and women, Italians and Germans, clergy and socialites.

Church authorities were not amused, and repeatedly censured Venetians for depicting holy subjects in an earthy Venetian light and for playing toe-tapping tunes in churches. But, in 1767, after persistent reproaches from Rome, Venice calculated the amount of revenue that it had rendered to Rome in the previous decade; the result was a grand total of 11 million golden ducats. Venice promptly closed 127 monasteries and convents, cutting the local clerical population by 50% and redirecting to the city's coffers millions of ducats that would otherwise have gone to Rome.

Meanwhile, Venetian tastes and trends stealthily took over drawing rooms across the continent, and the city became a playground for Europe's upper crust. Nunneries in Venice held soirées to rival those in its *ridotti* (casinos), and Carnevale lasted up to three months. Venetian 'white widows' with husbands at sea took young, handsome *cicisbei* (young manservants) to tend their needs. Not coincidentally, Venetian ladies also occasionally fell into religious fervours entailing a nine-month seclusion, and abandoned orphans soon filled four well-funded *ospedaletti* (orphanages). By the 18th century, less than 40% of Venetian nobles bothered with the formality of marriage, and the regularity of Venetian annulments scandalised even visiting French courtiers.

PARTY'S OVER

By the time Napoleon arrived in 1797, Venice had been reduced by plague and circumstance from 175,000 people to fewer than 100,000, and the Venetians' reputation as fierce partiers did nothing to prevent the French and Austrians from handing the city back and forth as a trophy. By 1817, one-quarter of Venice's population was destitute, and when Venice rallied to resist the Austrians in 1848–49, the Austrians' blockade left it wracked by cholera and short on food. The indignity of it all would fester until Venice joined the Kingdom of Italy in 1866.

The glamorous city took on a workaday aspect in the 19th and 20th centuries. Factories were added on Giudecca, a railway bridge was built, and Mussolini added a roadway from the mainland, literally bringing Venice into line with the rest of Italy. Venice capitulated to Fascism and Allied troops in turn, and the war and the shock of the mass deportation of the city's Jewish population in 1943–44 helped precipitate an urban identity crisis. By 1966, Venetians were abandoning the city for Milan and other postwar economic centres, and Venice seemed as forlorn as a party where invited guests had decided they had better things to do.

ALTA ACQUA

Then, on 4 November 1966, disaster struck. Record floods poured into 16,000 Venetian homes in terrifying waves, and residents were stranded in the wreckage of 1400 years of civilisation. But Venice refused to be mired in despair, instead calling on its many admirers for aid. Assistance poured in from Mexico to Australia, and from millionaires and pensioners alike; Unesco coordinated some 27 private organisations to redress the ravages of the flood. Photographs of the era (available online at www. albumdivenezia.it) show Venetians drying ancient books one page at a time, and gondolas gliding into bars for *spritz* (prosecco-based cocktails) served by bartenders in hip-high waders.

TOP FIVE FILMS SET IN VENICE

> *Pane e Tulipani (Bread and Tulips)* – An AWOL housewife starts life anew in Venice.
> *Casanova* – The story of the philanderer's life; watch the Fellini version with Donald Sutherland rather than Lasse Hallstrom's take (despite Heath Ledger's winsome presence).
> *Don't Look Now* – Julie Christie and Donald Sutherland's demons follow them to Venice in Nicolas Roeg's taut thriller.
> *Casino Royale* – The action-packed finale in this film takes James Bond down the Grand Canal (don't worry, that palace survived).
> *Death in Venice* – Luchino Visconti takes on Thomas Mann's story of a Mahler-esque composer, an infatuation and a deadly outbreak of disease.

NOALTRÍ V VOALTRÍ (US VERSUS THEM)

The usual outsider–insider dynamic doesn't quite wash in cosmopolitan Venice, whose excellent taste in imports ranges from Byzantine mosaics to the Venice Film Festival. Bringing a world-class art collection with you is one way to fit in, as Peggy Guggenheim and François Pinault discovered. But you don't have to be a mogul to *venexianárse* (become Venetian). Of the 20 million visitors to Venice each year, only some three million stay overnight; staying in a locally run B&B (p150) is a chance to experience Venice among Venetians. In addition, you can eat like a Venetian (p154), attempt a few words of Venetian dialect (p178) or learn a Venetian craft (p163). But the surest way to win over Venetians is to express curiosity about them and their city – so few day trippers stop to make polite conversation that any attempt is received with surprise and appreciation. As you'll soon find out, those other 17 million visitors are missing out on excellent company.

Venice's *alta acqua* (high-water) bravado may be its saving grace at a time when the population has continued to leave the city for the lower rents and job opportunities on the mainland, and cruise ships inundate the city with day trippers. But despite dire predictions, Venice has not yet become a Disneyland version of itself or a lost Atlantis. The city remains relevant and realistic, continuing to produce new music, art and crafts even as it seeks sustainable solutions to its rising water levels (p172). Venice today is anchored not merely by its ancient pylons, but by the people who put them there: the Venetians.

LIFE AS A VENETIAN

Look around: all those splendid palaces, paintings and churches were created by a handful of Venetians. In the city's entire history, there have only been about three million Venetians who could claim grandparents from Venice. With the 60,000 official residents easily outnumbered by visitors on any given day, Venetians may seem like a rarity in their own city. The population has halved in size since 1848, and 25% of the population is over 65. But there are 2000 children still playing tag in Venice's *campi* (squares), and local universities keep the city young and full of ideas. If you don't always encounter locals on the main thoroughfares it's because Venetians prefer to *andare per le fodere* (to go by the inner linings) of the city's 3000 backstreets.

Despite its reputation, this is not just a city of the idle rich. Most Venetians live in flats, and 1000 Venetian palaces are now used as hotels and

B&Bs. Hard-working Venetians pursue artisanal occupations that might sound esoteric: paper marbling, glass-blowing, octopus fishing. But they are constantly reinventing these traditions, and in tiny storefronts you can glimpse artisans turning paper into a purse, glass into jewellery, and baby octopuses into brilliant *cicheti* (Venetian tapas). Resting on past glories would be easy, while topping them seems impossible – but, as usual, Venetians are opting for the impossible.

ART

The sheer number of masterpieces packed into Venice might make you wonder if there's something in the water here. The reason may be more simple: historically, Venice tended not to starve its artists. Rather than suffering for their art, many Venetian artists and architects did quite well by it. So instead of dying young and destitute, painters such as Titian and Giovanni Bellini, and architects such as Jacopo Sansovino and Baldassare Longhena all survived into their eighties to produce late, great works. (For more on architecture, see p156.)

Venice's guild of house painters included some of art history's greatest names. One dues-paying member, Giovanni Bellini (c1430–1516), passed on his tremendous skills with human expression and glowing colour to two rather apt pupils: Giorgione (1477–1510) and Titian (c 1490–1576), whose work can be compared in the Accademia (p113). Vittore Carpaccio (1460–1526) rivalled Titian's reds with his own sanguine hues, but it was Titian's *Madonna of the Assumption* in I Frari (p84) that cemented Venice's reputation for glorious colour.

TOP FIVE BOOKS SET IN VENICE

> *Shakespeare in Venice* by Alberto Toso Fei – A captivating guide to the Venetian inspirations for Shakespeare's dramas, including *Othello* and *Merchant of Venice*.
> *The Passion* by Jeanette Winterson – Napoleon's cook pursues a card-dealing Venetian woman of mystery in this magic-realist fable.
> *History of Venice* by John Julius Norwich – A massive, engrossing epic, if a bit long on naval battles and short on recent history.
> *Corto Maltese: Fable of Venice* by Hugo Pratt – The Italian comic-book legend's cosmopolitan sea captain cracks the mysteries of the *calli* (streets).
> *Wings of the Dove* by Henry James – A con man and a sickly heiress meet in Venice, with a predictable outcome but gorgeous storytelling.

But though art history tends to insist on a division of labour between Venice and Florence – Venice had the colour, Florence the ideas – the Venetian school had plenty of ideas that repeatedly got it into trouble. Tintoretto may have earned key public commissions, but his lightning-bolt brushwork, which drew out human drama even in religious scenes, proved controversial. The luminous colours of Paolo Veronese (1528–88) were never in question, but his decision to depict Germans, Turks, gamblers and dogs among the saints in *The Last Supper* drew censure from the Church. He refused to change the picture, instead renaming it *Feast in the House of Levi*.

Pietro Longhi (1701–85) dispensed with the premise of lofty subject matter and painted Venetian social satires, while Giambattista Tiepolo (1696–1770) turned religious themes into a premise for dizzying ceilings covered with rococo sunbursts. Many Venetian artists turned their attention from the heavens to the local landscape, notably Canaletto (1697–1768). And, instead of drawing popes on thrones, portraitist Rosalba Carriera (1675–1757) captured her socialite sitters on snuffboxes.

ENVIRONMENT

With 400 bridges connecting 117 islets across 200 canals, Venice's natural setting is extraordinary – and extraordinarily fragile. The whole set-up is protected only by a slender arc of islands that halts the Adriatic's advances.

You may have heard that Venice is sinking, but that's not entirely accurate. The city is partially built on wooden foundations sunk deep into lagoon silt, and it's held up miraculously well for centuries. But the foundations are taking a pounding as never before, with new stresses coming from industrial pollutants and wakes of speeding motorboats. At the same time, the dredging of deeper channels to accommodate supertankers and cruise ships has contributed to the rise in water levels doubling since 1900. Back then, Piazza San Marco flooded about 10 times a year; now it's closer to 60. Technology advances have helped keep Venice afloat, and engineers now estimate that Venice may be able to withstand a 26cm to 60cm rise in water levels in the 21st century – which is great news, except for the fact that an intergovernmental panel on climate change recently forecasted increases as great as 88cm.

Complex solutions aren't easy, but simple gestures are. Recycling your waste and tidying as you go through Venice will be appreciated; when

TO MOSE, OR NOT TO MOSE?

The hot topic of the last 30 years in Venice has been a mobile-flood-barrier project known as MOSE. Ever since the great flood of 1966, many Unesco-affiliated agencies have been urgently concerned about this jewel box of a city, which contains many of the world's great art treasures, and MOSE proponents say the city must be saved at any cost.

Estimated at a cost of £1.5 billion, the 30m-high and 20m-wide inflatable barriers are intended to seal the three entrances to Venice's lagoon whenever the sea approaches dangerous levels. This is only a partial solution, however, since flooding is also caused by excessive rain and swollen inland rivers.

But, as many Venetians are quick to point out, the city is their home, not just a treasure chest, and the impact of any stop-gap measure must be considered. Would flood barriers fill the lagoon with stagnant water, creating public-health risks and driving away tourists? Could MOSE change local aquaculture and end fishing on the lagoon? Will it delay solutions to underlying problems?

The debate rages on as MOSE construction gets under way. Meanwhile, local environmentalists are keenly tracking the impact of global warming, cruise ships and pollution from the Marghera petrochemical plant on water levels, fishing prospects and everyday life in Venice.

receptacles are scarce or full, take your rubbish with you. Spare the city the effort of recycling some 20 to 60 million water bottles annually by insisting on tap water. Gondoliers will sing your praises if you ask water-taxi drivers to go slower to avoid kicking up a wake. Spend time and money in locally owned businesses, and you'll be assuring your Venetian hosts that all their effort to maintain the city is worthwhile.

DIRECTORY
TRANSPORT
ARRIVAL & DEPARTURE

AIR

Most flights arrive on the mainland at **Marco Polo Airport** (VCE; ☎ 041 2609260; www.veniceairport.it), 12km from Venice. Low-cost airlines are a benefit to travellers, but a burden on the environment and Venice's air quality; to travel with a cleaner conscience, consider a carbon-offset program (see below).

See p174 for information on getting to/from the airport.

TRAIN

Prompt, affordable, scenic and environmentally friendly, trains are an excellent way to travel to and from Venice. Trains run frequently to Venice's Stazione Santa Lucia (signed as Ferrovia within Venice) from major European cities and

locations throughout Italy, and all vaporetti (city ferries) stop right outside the station. Tickets for all trains can be purchased at self-serve ticketing machines in the station, online at www.trenitalia .it, or at **Rail Europe** (☎ 0844 8484064; www.raileurope.co.uk) in the UK.

GETTING AROUND

Major destinations within Venice are rarely more than a 10- to 30-minute walk away, not including photo and gelato pit stops. **Azienda Consorzio Trasporti Veneziano** (ACTV; www.actv.it) organises the vaporetto network that runs inside Venice and to outlying islands, including Giudecca, Lido, Murano, Burano and Torcello. In this book, the nearest vaporetto stop is noted after the 🚤 in each listing.

TRAVEL PASSES

If you're planning to use public transport often, buy a **biglietto a**

CLIMATE CHANGE & TRAVEL

Travel – especially air travel – is a significant contributor to global climate change. At Lonely Planet, we believe that all who travel have a responsibility to limit their personal impact. As a result, we have teamed with Rough Guides and other concerned industry partners to support Climate Care, which allows people to offset the greenhouse gases they are responsible for with contributions to energy-saving projects and other climate-friendly initiatives in the developing world. Lonely Planet offsets all staff and author travel.

For more information, turn to the responsible travel pages on www.lonelyplanet .com. For details on offsetting your carbon emissions and a carbon calculator, go to www .climatecare.org.

TRAVEL TO/FROM THE AIRPORT

	Ferry	ATVO Fly Bus	ACTV bus 5	Water taxi
Pick-up point	at the dock, located a 10min walk from terminal	in front of terminal	in front of terminal	at the dock, located a 10min walk from terminal
Drop-off point	docks including Fondamente Nuove, San Marco and Zattere	Piazzale Roma	Piazzale Roma	nearest dock to hotel
Duration	1¼hr	20min	40min	30-50min, depending on destination
Cost	€13	€3	€1	depends on destination and number of passengers; usually €90-120 for 4 people
Other	purchase tickets in terminal or at dock	departs every 30-50min; purchase tickets at Piazzale Roma or the terminal	makes frequent mainland stops; purchase tickets at Piazzale Roma or the terminal	you can sometimes book with other hotel guests; ask at front desk
Contact	www.alilaguna.com	www.atvo.it	www.actv.it	☎ 041 5222303, 041 5221265

tempo (24-/72-hr ticket €16/31), a timed ticket that allows unlimited access to all transport (except the Alilaguna, Clodia, Fusina and LineaBlù services) for 24 or 72 hours from the first validation. Tickets can be purchased at ACTV ticket booths at vaporetti stops.

VeniceCard (☎ 041 2424; www.hello venezia.com; transport & culture pass junior/senior 3-day €50.50/59, 7-day €57/58; ☎ call centre 8am-7.30pm) offers a three-day or seven-day transport and culture pass that entitles holders to unlimited use of vaporetti during the given period, plus free entry to civic museums and discounts on church entry, cultural events and special exhibitions. Venicecard can be purchased at the **Azienda di Promozione Turistica Office** (APT; Map pp42-3, G5; ☎ 041 5298711; www.turismo venezia.it; Piazza San Marco 71f, San Marco; ☺ 9am-3.30pm Mon-Sat) in San Marco; at helloVenezia ticket outlets at **Stazione Santa Lucia** (Map pp72-3, B5; Cannaregio; ☺ 7am-8.30pm), **Ferrovia vaporetto stop** (Map pp72-3, B5; Cannaregio) and **Piazzale Roma** (Map pp100-1, B3; Santa Croce); or at a 15% discount online at www.hellovenezia.com/jsp/it/venicecard/index.jsp.

For travellers aged 15 to 29, **Rolling VeniceCard** (pass €4) allows you to buy a 72-hour public-transport pass for €18 and provides discounted access to monuments and cultural events. The pass can be purchased at helloVenezia ticket booths; identification is required.

VAPORETTO

Several vaporetto lines run up and down the Grand Canal, some with faster *limitato* (limited-stop) service. Line 1 makes all stops between Ferrovia and San Marco in about 30 to 45 minutes. Tickets should be bought in advance and validated prior to boarding in the yellow machines located dockside. Single-trip tickets cost €6.50, so travel passes (above) offer good value. Timetables are available online at www.actv.it/english/home.php and are posted at stops; next departures are often listed at the stops on digital displays. Some lines start as early as 5.30am, while others stop as early as 9pm. A night (N) service runs along the Grand Canal and serves the Lido and Giudecca, but all services stop at 4.30am.

TRAGHETTO

Get your gondola ride on the cheap. Both picturesque and practical, *traghetti* are large commuter gondolas that cross the Grand Canal at set spots for €1 per passenger. But there are no seats – everyone crosses standing. Some operate from about 9am to 6pm, while others stop at around noon. Look for *traghetto* signs on *calli* (streets) parallel to the Grand Canal.

GONDOLA

More than a way to get from point A to point B, a gondola trip is an insight into a hidden Venice that is anything but pedestrian, offering rare peeks into *palazzi* (palaces or mansions) and courtyards. Official rates for 40 minutes are €80 during the day or €100 from 7pm to 8am, not including opera arias (negotiated separately) or tips. Additional time is charged in 20-minute increments (day/night €40/50). You may be offered a price break in overcast weather or around midday, when other travellers are too hot and hungry for gondola rides. Agree in advance on a price, time limit and singing to avoid surcharges.

Gondolas cluster at *stazi* (stops) along the Grand Canal and near major monuments (including I Frari, Ponte dei Sospiri and Gallerie dell'Accademia), but you can also book one by phoning ☎ 041 5285075.

WATER TAXI

The James Bond way to get around town is on these sleek teak

DIRECTORY

RECOMMENDED MODES OF TRANSPORT

	Stazione Santa Lucia	Rialto	Ghetto
Stazione Santa Lucia	n/a	line 1 vaporetto 15min	walk 10min
Rialto	line 1 vaporetto 15min	n/a	walk 20min
Ghetto	walk 10min	walk 20min	n/a
Gallerie dell'Accademia	line 3 vaporetto 15min	walk 20min	line 82 vaporetto 20min
Piazza San Marco	line 3 vaporetto 25min	walk 15min	line 82 vaporetto 30min
Zanipolo	line 41/51 vaporetto 30min	walk 15min	line 42/52 vaporetto 20min

speedboats. Official rates start at €8.90, plus €1.80 per minute, €6 extra if the boat is called to your hotel, and more for night trips, luggage and large groups – so even short trips run from €60 to €90. But with unwieldy luggage or a group of 10 to 20, a water taxi may be the best way to reach your destination. Taxis are metered, but prices can also be negotiated in advance; a trip from Rialto to San Marco should cost around €60. You can book a water taxi by calling either ☎ 041 5222303 or ☎ 041 2406711.

Ignore water-taxi drivers at Piazzale Roma who claim there are no vaporetti stops nearby; the stops are in front of the bus terminal.

BUS
Buses run from Piazzale Roma (Map pp100–1, B4) to Mestre and other mainland destinations, as well as up and down the Lido.

Tickets cost €1 (or €9 for 10 rides) at news-stands or tobacconists, and are good for an hour once validated in the machine on the bus. Schedules are posted at most stops and online at www.actv.it.

PRACTICALITIES
BUSINESS HOURS
Hours during August and winter may vary, but businesses are usually open from 9am to 1pm and 3.30pm to 7.30pm Monday to Saturday. Restaurants and cafes are usually open Sunday and may be closed Monday or Tuesday. See inside front cover for more-specific opening hours.

DISCOUNTS
Chorus pass (☎ 041 2750462; www .chorusvenezia.org; adult/child/family €8/6/18) offers single entry to 16 Venetian churches and is valid for one year; it's for sale at

Gallerie dell'Accademia	Piazza San Marco	Zanipolo
line 3 vaporetto 15min	line 3 vaporetto 25min	line 41/51 vaporetto 30min
walk 20min	walk 15min	walk 15min
line 82 vaporetto 20min	line 82 vaporetto 30min	line 42/52 vaporetto 20min
n/a	walk 15min	walk 30min
walk 15min	n/a	walk 15min
walk 30min	walk 15min	n/a

ticket booths at the participating churches.

The **Museum pass** (www.museiciviciveneziani.it; adult/child €18/12) is valid for single entry to 11 museums over six months; a more limited ticket offers entry to the five museums around Piazza San Marco for €12/6.50 per adult/child. The pass is available at the tourist office (p179).

See p174 for information on VeniceCard and Rolling VeniceCard.

HOLIDAYS

1 January	New Year's Day
6 January	Epiphany
March/April	Good Friday
March/April	Easter Monday
25 April	Liberation Day
1 May	Labour Day
15 August	Feast of the Assumption
1 November	All Saints' Day
8 December	Feast of the Immaculate Conception
25 December	Christmas Day
26 December	Boxing Day

INTERNET

To find out what's doing in Venice, check out these useful websites:

A Guest in Venice (www.aguestinvenice.com) Hotelier association provides information on upcoming exhibitions, events and lectures.

Guardian Travel (www.guardian.co.uk /travel/venice) The UK paper and its readers offer tips on travel that's last minute, on the cheap, with dogs, and more.

Italy Magazine (www.italymag.co.uk/italy_re gions/veneto_friuli_trentino/) Accommodation website provides info on language and cookery schools, as well as accommodation listings.

Save Venice (www.savevenice.org)

Slow Travel Italy (www.slowtrav.com/italy) Offers accommodation and restaurant listings, trip-planning tips and forums to connect with other travellers.

Venezia da Vivere (www.veneziadavivere .com) This is *the* guide to what's hip and happening in Venice now; it lists music performances, art openings, nightlife, new designers and more.

Venice Explorer (http://veniceexplorer.net) Provides listings and locator maps for Venice's restaurants, shops and attractions.

Venice Tourist Board (www.turismovenezia .it) This site sells tickets to major city attractions; it also covers upcoming cultural events.
Weekend a Venezia (http://en.venezia.waf .it) Discounted and last-minute tickets to major tourist attractions.

The following are a selection of Venice's internet cafes:
Internet Point San Barnaba (Map pp110–11, D3; ☎ 041 2770926; Campo San Barnaba 2759, Dorsoduro; internet 20min €3; ⏰ 9am-1.30pm & 3.30-7pm Mon-Sat)
Net Gate (Map pp72-3, D2; ☎ 041 2440213; Crosera San Pantalon, Dorsoduro; internet 1hr €8; ⏰ 9.30am-7pm Mon-Sat)
VeNice (Map pp72-3, B5; ☎ 041 2758217; Rio Terà Lista di Spagna 149, Cannaregio; internet 30min €3; ⏰ 9am-11pm)
World House (Map pp60–1, B3; ☎ 041 5284871; www.world-house.org; Calle della Chiesa 4502, Castello; internet 1hr/3hr €8/18; ⏰ 10am-11pm)

LANGUAGE

A few choice words in Venetian will endear you to your hosts, especially at happy hour. To keep up with the *bacaro* (bar) banter, try mixing these phrases in with your Italian:

Cheers!	*Sanacapána!*
cheap wine	*brunbrún*
glass (of wine)	*ombra*
happy hour	*giro di ombra*
How lucky!	*Bénpo!*
It's all the same to me.	*De rufe o de rafe.*
Oh no!	*Siménteve!*
Perfect.	*In bróca.*
to become Venetian	*venexianárse*
to carouse	*far el samartinéto*
Watch out!	*Ócio!*
Welcome!	*Benvegnú!*
Yes sir!	*Siorsi!*
You bet!	*Figurárse!*
you guys	*voaltrí*
Venetian (m/f)	*venexiano/a*

MONEY

Italy uses the euro (€); see inside front cover for exchange rates.

Your accommodation will be your main expense in Venice, followed by meals, which start at €2 to €3 for a couple of *cicheti* (Venetian tapas) or a slice of pizza – although the sky's the limit at Harry's Bar. An *ombra* (glass) of wine or prosecco runs to €1.50 to €3, and espresso at the bar costs €0.80 to €1. Instead of buying bottled water, you can save money and the environment with a glass of mineral water at the bar for €0.20 to €0.50. When your feet get tired, hop on the vaporetto for €6.50. At €80 for 40 minutes, a gondola ride is not a means of transport – it's a main event, and a memorable way to explore the canals.

TELEPHONE

GSM and tri-band mobile phones can be used in Italy with a local SIM card; these can be purchased at Vodafone and Telecom Italia Mobile outlets across the city. Coin-operated orange Telecom Italia phone booths can be found around major piazzas.

COUNTRY & CITY CODES

When calling Venetian landlines, even from within the city, you must dial the ☎ 041 city code; local mobile numbers have no initial 0. To call from outside Italy, first dial the Italian country code (☎ 39).

USEFUL PHONE NUMBERS

See inside front cover for a list of useful phone numbers, including emergency numbers and directory assistance.

....

TIPPING

It is customary to leave a 10% tip at restaurants where service is not included in the bill, and you can leave small change at cafes. Hotel porters are tipped €0.50 per bag.

TOURIST INFORMATION

Venice has tourist offices run by **Azienda di Promozione Turistica** (APT; ☎ 041 5298711; www.turismovenezia.it) at a number of locations:
Marco Polo Airport (9.30am-7.30pm) In the arrivals hall.
Piazza San Marco (Map pp42-3, G5; Piazza San Marco 71f, San Marco; 9am-3.30pm Mon-Sat) Venice's main tourism office.
Piazzale Roma (Map pp100-1, B3; Santa Croce; 9.30am-1pm & 1.30-4.30pm)
Stazione Santa Lucia (Map pp72-3, B5; Cannaregio; 8am-6.30pm)

TRAVELLERS WITH DISABILITIES

A **disabled-assistance office** (Map pp72-3, B5; Stazione Santa Lucia, Cannaregio; 7am-9pm) is located in front of platform 4 at Stazione Santa Lucia. For further information on accessibility in Venice, try **Informahandicap** (Map pp42-3, G5; ☎ 041 2748144; www .comune.venezia.it/informahandicap, in Italian; San Marco; 3-5pm Wed).

>INDEX

See also separate subindexes for See (p188), Shop (p189), Eat (p190), Drink (p191) and Play (p191).

000 map pages

000 map pages

🍴 EAT

000 map pages

000 map pages